AND THEN...
EVERYTHING
CHANGED

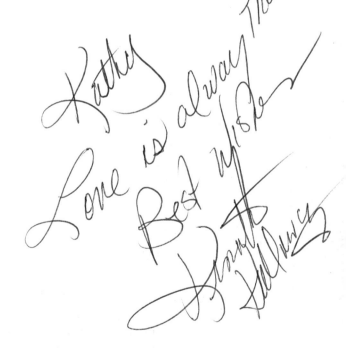

Kathy
Love is always true!
Best wishes
Kinnith Holloway

KINNITH HOLLOWAY

outskirtspress

DENVER, COLORADO

This book is dedicated to my wife, Debbie Holloway,
my children, Tiffany, Kenneth and A.J.

To my loving parents,
Webster and Anna Holloway
'Without You There Is No Me"

Prologue

It was never my intention to write a book. In fact, the whole process has been a very difficult struggle. I have had many requests to write my conversion story over the years, yet I resisted. In 2004, a close friend of mine told me I was being selfish by not sharing my story with others. I only resisted because I did not feel this was a story that anyone would care to read. However, the Lord thought otherwise.

The Lord got my undivided attention and compelled me to write my conversion story. And this is it.

"Blessed be the name of the Lord from this time forth and for evermore." Psalms 113:2 (KJV)

Chapter 1

Day 1

It was a typical summer day. The date was August 26. It was early in the morning and everything was going fine. All of our family was in good health. We were not particularly worried about anything. We were just living life. Debbie and I got up to get ready to go to work as usual. It was just a pleasant day, there was nothing special about it. Debbie and I ate breakfast, read the scriptures, had prayer and got dressed to go to work. We went downstairs and got into the car. I started the car and we talked about what we needed to do that evening. I backed out of the garage and made a left turn onto the street. We headed toward the main road. I made a left turn onto the main street and noticed that there was a police officer behind me with his lights flashing. I knew I was not speeding. I wondered why the police officer would be stopping me. The police officer came to my window. I got my insurance papers and driver's license out of the glove compartment. The officer asked for my license. Debbie cautioned me, "Do not say anything." We did not know how it was in Utah, but in Louisiana, a black man and the police did not mix. Therefore, I heeded her warning and said nothing. The officer took my license and registration and went to his car. The officer came back to my car and asked me to get out of the car because he needed to speak with me. I got out of the car and went to speak to the officer at the back of my car.

The most out-of-the-blue thing happened at that point! The officer said to me, "I have a warrant for your arrest." Stunned, I said, "For what?" The police officer said that it was a warrant from the state of Louisiana and he had to take me to jail. I asked, "Are you kidding me?" He replied, "I am not kidding, sir, and I have to put you in handcuffs." I thought this had to be some kind of a joke or a case of mistaken identity. I grew up in the south. There, it is said that all black people look alike. This time I was hoping for the statement to be true. The officer said, "Turn around and put your hands behind your back." Now this was getting very serious. I realized that this was not a joke. I was being arrested! I turned around. I then placed my hands behind my back. I felt the handcuff on my right wrist click. Then the handcuff on my left wrist clicked. Now I knew how handcuffs felt! Let me tell you, it was not a very good feeling! The police officer said, "You seem like a good guy, I am sure this is nothing and you should be out of jail tomorrow". "Tomorrow?" I asked. You have to be kidding, I thought. I have too many things to do to be gone that long. I thought about my job, my Master's program, my church calling, my wife, and my son on a mission. This couldn't be happening to me.

However, it was happening to me! My mind was working at a thousand miles per second looking for answers. The police officer placed me in the back seat of his patrol car. The back seat was a very tight fit. There were no door controls in the back of the police officer's car. There was no way to open the door or let down the windows. Then I thought I have to give Debbie my credit cards and some instruction as to what needed to be done to get me out of this nightmare. I asked the police officer, "May I speak with my wife, please?" The officer answered, "Yes, you can." The police officer let me out of the back seat of the patrol car and I went to speak with Debbie. Debbie was about to cry. I told her, "You will have to be strong because you are the only one who can get me out of this mess." I gave her the credit cards and some instructions. "The problem is, I have no idea why I am being arrested or how to get out of this mess since I have no clue what this mess is." This was such a helpless feeling, but there was nothing I could do at the moment. The police officer escorted me back to his car. He opened the door and I got into the back seat. The handcuffs were hurting my wrists. I was so uncomfortable in the back of this patrol car. I began thinking, this is incredible, of all places, and I am in Utah where there are only 100 black people. Now here I am, a black person, sitting in the back seat of a police car in handcuffs. I am doing a great job of representing my race. Man, how could such a perfect day deteriorate to this point? I had definitely not planned to do this today. No one would ever believe this. I didn't believe it myself.

Now we were on our way to the... I didn't know where! At that point, I heard the officer speaking to someone on his radio and he told someone that he was on his way to Spanish Fork. I had only been to Spanish Fork once since I moved to Utah. I asked the officer, "Where are we going?" He said, "to Utah County Jail." Thank goodness that I told Debbie the right place. So as we were driving the officer began to ask me questions. Like where are you from? I told him I was from Mississippi, but I moved here from Louisiana. The officer said, "You don't sound like you know anything about this. You don't seem like a person that would purposely do something like this." My response was, "Something like what?" The police office answered, "I am not sure." His statement was true, but here I was in the back of a police car, handcuffed, not knowing why I was being arrested and on my way to jail. I thought that maybe I had done something wrong, but what? I was racking my brain, searching for something, anything that I could have done wrong. There were some things I had done, but nothing that would get me arrested. The police officer continued to drive toward the Utah County Jail. I tried again. I asked the officer, "Do you know what is on the warrant?" He hesitated. Then he groaned and said, "You know I am really not supposed to do this. But you seem like you really have no clue as to what this is about." The police officer glanced at the papers and said, "The warrant is for fraud and larceny." I thought, larceny, what is larceny? This whole thing was crazy. However, I had to find a way out of this. As we continued down the interstate, I couldn't believe this was happening. It seemed like a dream. We talked as the police officer drove for about twenty-five minutes. The officer kept saying, "You don't seem like you would do anything wrong. This must be a mistake." I was thinking, "Then why don't you just let me go?"

Right in front of me, I could see the Utah County Jail complex. It looked like a prison. We drove up to the gate. This was not a chain-link fence, but a large metal wall that rolled back to allow a car to enter the jail grounds. Once I saw what was behind the gate, I knew it was a jail. There would be no way for me to leave. My heart gave way to feelings of depression, hopelessness, loneliness, loss, regret and no peace. How could this be true? However, here I was, so it had to be true. Not all of my physical and mental strength and cunning could get me out of this situation. It looked like I was going to have to go through it, whatever it was. This was a tough situation. Yet my heart cried out for Debbie. "What could I do to help her?" She couldn't be alone in Utah! Debbie was far away from her home, family and familiar surroundings. The purpose of my life was to protect her! Now I couldn't. I had lost one of my life's battles. I prayed to God to protect her, "Give her strength, Father." For at this moment I didn't know when or where I would see her again.

The police officer stopped the car. The car was in the belly of the jail compound. The police officer let me out of the car and took me to a large open room. It appeared to be where they processed prisoners. I couldn't believe I was a prisoner. There were two officers at this counter. They asked me to step forward and checked me for weapons. There was one black and one white male officer. They were both very nice people. They took the handcuffs off, took all of my belongings, placed them in a bag, and sealed the bag. One of the officers asked me, "Are you from Louisiana?" I stated that I lived there for about nine years. The police officer said that he was from Alexandria, LA.

We discussed food as he continued to check me into the jail. Then he said, "Louisiana will not come this far to pick you up. You could be in jail for a while." This did not make me feel good. After checking my pockets, the police officer had me sit and wait for more processing. While sitting there on a bench, I wondered what was next. How was Debbie holding up? My mind went through thousands of things in those 15 minutes. However, I still had no idea why I was here. I did not know who was behind the warrant. I had left so many enemies in Baton Rouge. Most of my enemies I did not even know! However, I believe there were a lot of them.

Then I heard this horrible sound. "Holloway come with me," stated the guard. I knew this was the time for me to be locked up. I asked the Lord to let me remember my military training. Please, let me remember my football training for it appeared to me that I would need to rely on those experiences. I went with the guard. He was a very nice man. He asked me to hold out my left arm. I held out my arm and he attached a bracelet to my wrist. My picture, name, date of birth and a bar code was on this band. I knew I was trapped with nowhere to run and no way out. My words, education, and street smarts wouldn't get me out of this place now. I wanted my mom, my brothers, my sisters, my children, and my wife, yet there was no one but me. I was alone in this battle, all the time knowing I couldn't win from within the jail. I needed help from the outside world!

The guard took me to a doctor. This doctor was also a nice man. He examined me and stated that I was in the best health he had seen in a long time. This was nice to know yet it would not get me out of jail. He finished and gave me a phone card. He said I could make a phone call. Little did I know, but this doctor gave me the first sign of hope; access to the outside world. I called Debbie. She was holding up okay. I told her to call Larry, an attorney in Baton Rouge, to see if he could find out what was going on. I gave Debbie other instructions and told her I should be out tomorrow since I was going to court at that time. My plan was to post bail, then fly to Baton Rouge to clear up this matter. Now the phone call was about 3 minutes long. This was all the time I had to talk. It seemed all calls have to go through a phone system. I had to use the calling card to make the call and Debbie's cell number was long distance. This was because we never changed our phone numbers from Louisiana. Therefore, my call could only be three minutes since it was long distance. That did not matter. I had to put into motion a plan to get me out of jail.

After sitting in this lobby area for about an hour, the police officer told me to go with a guy who was just passing by. I got up from my chair and followed him. This person took me to a room. This room had a counter in the back portion of the room. There was another guy behind this counter. There was a large storage room behind this counter. I went up to the counter and the officer asked, "What size underwear? What size shirt? What size shoes?" I gave him my sizes. He went into the storage room and came back with these items. He told me to undress and put the clothes on that he had brought me. I undressed and put on the clothes he brought to me. Then, he took my clothes, put them into a bag, and sealed it. Now here I was wearing all of their clothes, an orange jumpsuit with orange slippers. This was very different. Yet, I served eight years in the military, four of which were overseas. I could handle this. However, I worried so much for Debbie.

The guards were taking me to my cell now. Four others were being escorted to their jail cells along with me. We were walking down a long hallway. I was to be locked up in a holding area until I could meet with someone who decided on my more permanent location. A big door to my right slid open with a bang! The guard told me to enter this area. Others went further down the hallway. This hallway was about eight-feet wide. The guard stopped me and said, "This is your bay." I went into the bay area. I checked in with the guards at this location. The guard told me to get a mattress pad and a sheet.

This sheet was made with an opening on one side. This allowed the mattress to slide into the sheet that looked like a large bag. The guard assigned me to a small bay. This bay had six sets of bunk beds, so it could sleep 12 people. The bay had a sliding see-through door and the whole bay had a glass front about 20 feet long. The other three walls were cement block walls. There was a shower room. The commode was behind a four-foot long wall. The bathroom had three sides and the open side was directed toward the guard station. It was so that the guard could see into bathroom. There was very little privacy. I had a bottom bunk and this was where I was to sleep. There were guys telling stories about what they had done to be in jail. Eighty percent of the inmate's issues were drug-related. The guard then allowed me to make a phone call. I called Debbie to inform her of my status. I had been told that I would go to court the next day. I ate dinner. It was okay. It was not home, but now it was time to go to bed. I was the only black person I could see at this moment. About an hour later, I was able to see all of the inmates in this bay. The population I saw was about 100 inmates. There were three blacks, and they were in another bay with maybe ten Hispanics. Everyone else was white, unbelievable. I lay in bed. Looking around to be sure, I was prepared for anything strange that might happen during the night. "Lord, please protect me," I prayed. Tomorrow I was headed to court. I would just post bail, get out of jail, and fly to Louisiana. Once I was in Louisiana, I would pay whatever was needed and this would be over. Goodnight!

Chapter 2

I was born in Prentiss, Mississippi in the heart of the Bible Belt. I grew up in a little town called Moss Point about five miles from the Gulf of Mexico. I grew up very close to the beach. I lived in a household where everybody was very religious. My mom was a member of the Church of God in Christ, which is sort of like a Pentecostal church or Holiness type of church. My dad belonged to the Methodist church. I had five brothers and three sisters. Some of my siblings were Baptist, some were Pentecostal and others did not go to church.

Every Sunday morning, no matter what you did, you would get up and go to church. I went to church with my mother most of the time where I heard many things about Jesus Christ and God. The people would "shout," which consisted of physically jumping around wildly while simultaneously speaking different praises unto the name of the Lord. This "shouting" is explained as how a body reacts when the Holy Spirit is upon it. There were actually a group of women in the church that were called the "hallelujah" group. They would get up and repeatedly say hallelujah while this "shouting" was happening. There were others that only walked back and forth while expressing thanks unto the name of the Lord. On Sunday morning, my mom would get up and go to her church, my dad would get up and go to his church, and my sisters and brothers would get up and go to their church. As I said, I went to church with my mom most of the time. Surprisingly, one day my mother came to me, when I was about twelve years old, and said to me, "Son, you are twelve years old and that is old enough for you to decide which church you want to attend. You can go with your Father or you can go with your sisters and brothers or you can go with me." In the Bible, twelve was the age at which Jesus was found teaching in the synagogue. This is why my mother made this statement. I thought that this was somewhat peculiar. Because I thought that all churches were the same because everyone had the same Bible. In my thinking, I saw the Bible as a manual. I believed it would not matter where I decided to go because all of the churches had the same manual. This manual consisted of an Old Testament and a New Testament! You see I did not know that there was a difference between the churches or denominations. Therefore, I really did not quite understand exactly what she was asking me to decide. What she was saying was that I had become old enough to make my own decision about what I believed. I decided that I did not really want to go to any church. At certain times of the year, I stayed at home and watched football more than I would attend church. Yet when I did attend church, I would go to my mom or dad's church or my sister's and brother's church. My decision was really based on which church had the prettiest girls because I had no interest in religion whatsoever. I was not sure about the idea of Jesus Christ and God.

I had begun to grow up and reached the age of fifteen. I became more definitive about my thoughts and my feelings concerning religion. I did not understand nor did I believe that this guy named Jesus Christ died for my sins. I did not believe that somehow we could be forgiven and somehow go to a place called Heaven. I did not believe in a place called hell. It appeared to me that most people wanted to go to Heaven only because they did not want to go to hell. It seemed like hell was a place you would go and would burn in some kind of eternal fire. Then Heaven was the opposite, but no one seemed to have any idea what was to happen in Heaven. So who would want to burn in hell? I felt that people chose Heaven because it was believed that you would not burn there.

I remember one of the first experiences that I had with a minister. My uncle was a minister. I came home one day, and he was under the shade tree drinking a beer. I walked up to him and said, "Uncle Elijah, why are you drinking a beer? I do not think preachers should drink beer." Uncle Elijah said, "Son, let me tell you something. You do what I say, not what I do!" I was confused by this. I believed my uncle was closer to God than anybody, except my mom. Yet he was saying something conflicting to me. The idea of doing what someone said, compared to what they did, did not work for me. If you were going to follow this idea or this concept of God, then you had to do what the Bible said. I did not really believe the Bible anyway, but it seemed to me if you were going to be a follower of Jesus Christ, then you needed to do your best to follow the teachings found in the Bible.

Time went on and I remember a minister came to our town once claiming to be some sort of healer. I went to the church where he preached. He told people to come to the front of the church because he was going to heal them of whatever ailed them. My brother went up to the front and the guy put his hands on my brother's head. All of a sudden, my brother began to choke as if he could not swallow. The minister said, "Nobody move! Somebody close the church doors! Everybody get on your knees and start praying!" He said a demon was coming out of my brother. Something did come out of his mouth. It was some type of wet-looking object. It almost looked like vomit. I am not sure to this day what it was, but when it hit the floor, it dissipated or dissolved. Everyone was running, screaming, and crying, 'Oh, God.' The preacher kept saying, "Get on your knees and pray... make it so the demon will not go inside you!" I watched this and I thought, what the heck just happened. There was this concept of demons being inside of people.

I had many religious experiences, yet I did not have any concept or any idea of what these things meant. I knew someone named God and someone named Jesus Christ and I knew that somehow Jesus Christ was God's son. Jesus died on the cross for the sins of all people. I was not sure why He would do this. Somehow, He was supposed to save us and I guess that would be saving us from hell. I recall years later when I was around sixteen or so. I was playing football and I had this very close friend named Jerry. One day, Jerry showed up at practice and he said he was not going to play football anymore because it conflicted with going to church. I thought, what! What happened was that Jerry was at church and something happened in the church and he became what they called "saved." I was not sure what saved meant, but somehow, you "caught" the Holy Ghost. This Holy Ghost came upon you and changed you and you did not do the things that you did before. Therefore, football was not a priority for him anymore. He stopped playing football completely. Now I admired him for what he was doing. He was doing something that he believed. I do believe, however, that this move cost our team a state championship! That was my only concern at the time. But, Jerry continued to go to church. I admired him because he followed what he believed and that was fine with me. I did not quite understand it, but it was okay.

Some time later, I went to my first music concert in Mobile, Alabama. I saw a group called Brick. When Brick was performing a particular song, all of the people in the audience began to sweat and they began to move in a certain way as if they were slightly drunk. These people began to fall down and pass out. I had seen this behavior before. I began to think that… is it possible that the Holy Ghost that I have heard so much about could be at this concert. When the concert was over, I remember going home and talking to my mom. I asked her, "Mom is it possible that the Holy Ghost could have been at this concert?" She said, "No, this concert thing that you went to… that is of the devil!" And I remember saying, "But mom the expressions and the responses of the people were exactly the same as what

I have seen in church! These people at the concert were behaving the same way as a person that was being visited by the Holy Ghost." My Mom said, "You have said enough and do not speak that way again." That is how it was in the South. When your mother says that is enough, it is enough. So I held my tongue and walked away from her, but I was really confused and thinking that I didn't understand this Holy Ghost stuff. Even more, I absolutely did not understand any of this religious stuff. I did not know what was going on. Therefore, I began to separate myself from the whole concept of Christianity, the Bible, God and Jesus Christ. I was put in a position where I could not ask the questions I needed answered from the people I trusted. I could not ask my mom. She looked at these questions as blasphemy.

So in the middle of the Bible Belt, all of my brothers and sisters had an idea of religion and what it is all about, but I didn't. I just totally did not understand what it was all about. It was not that I did not believe in the concept of God. I believed there was some type of super power that created and controlled everything in the universe. However, I did not know what that power was and I was not sure that this Christian God was truly that power.

I remember my dad telling me, "Son, when you turn eighteen and graduate from high school you are going to have to move out of my house because two men cannot live in the same house." I thought that was kind of interesting. I really did not believe what he was say-ing, but I did think it was interesting. Well, when I figured out that he was serious I knew that when I graduated from high school I was go-ing to have to move out. Going to college was the route that I would choose to go. During my high school years, I had a girlfriend and we had a daughter. Sometimes, I went to church with my girlfriend. Her name was Kathy. I was at her church once and I heard the minister preaching. I thought it was bizarre the things he was saying. I began to raise my hand to tell him that what he was saying was not what the Bible said. I had begun to read the Bible a little bit and I always felt uncomfortable when the minister would talk about things that were not in the Bible. She stopped me. Needless to say, she never took me to church with her again! I did not know that I was not supposed to question the minister. Whatever he taught in the sermon was just the way it was because he was a man of God. If the man of God said something, that was the way it was and you should not question it nor should you question God. This was just the way it was. This was what our parents believed. I totally rejected that concept because if God wanted to know me, and He wanted me to know Him, somehow we had to communicate with each other. But I grew up in an environment where you could not communicate with this God. Therefore, I rejected the Christian concept and went on with my life doing whatever I wanted to do because I did not believe in Christianity.

Chapter 3

Day 2

finally fell asleep around 1 am. It is hard to sleep when you are not sure of your surroundings, if you know what I mean! After a few hours of sleep, I heard my name being called. I am not sure, but it must have been around 5:00 am. I was not sure why the guard was calling my name! Why were they calling me? Then the guard shouted, "Holloway! Get up and get dressed. You are going to court!" I got up from bed and begin to get dressed. All of the guys who were in the cell with me wished me luck. You see these guys knew I did not belong in jail. Most of these guys had been in jail many times and understood how the jail system worked. I finished putting on my clothes, brushed my teeth and waited for the cell door to open. The cell door opened by sliding to my right and I walked out of the cell. The guard told me to go down a short hallway and another guard would be waiting. I went down the hallway and another bigger sliding door opened. I was in a big hallway. I realized that this was the way I came in yesterday. The guard told me to go across this hallway to another hallway. Now I was standing in a hallway about 25 yards long and four feet wide. There was no one there but me and maybe six guards. All of these guards had handcuffs and guns.

Then, all of a sudden, I heard a lot of voices. There were people cursing and saying lots of sexual things. Then, I saw them. There were maybe 35 men that showed up in the hallway with me. We were in a line that stretched the length of the hallway. Then a group of women came down the hallway. The guys began to say things to the women like, "What's your name?" The guys said other vulgar things I will not write. Most of the women, which was about 10, reacted as if they enjoyed the attention. One of women spoke to me. She seemed to be nice and asked me a few questions. You see I was the only black person and she wondered how I ended up at this location. I told her a few things. I knew not to say much because she didn't have the need to know much about me.

The guards stated, "Turn around and face the wall." They searched all of us. After the search, I knew it was time to put on the handcuffs. Then I got a surprise! The guards said, "Lift your left foot." I did and he put the cuffs on my left and then right ankle. There was a chain connecting the two cuffs that was about eighteen inches long. Then the guard told me to turn around. I did. Then he put cuffs on my wrists. I thought of my slave ancestors. How they must have felt with little to no chance of escape once the cuffs were on! I wanted to cry but I knew where I was and knew what I had to do. I said a short prayer that I could think and feel just like I did when I was in the military. Immediately, my mind took me back to my military days and this mindset strengthened me. In the military, I spent a lot of time in places that were not good for humans to be! During those times, your mind was your best ally.

Now that all of us are chained and cuffed, the guard told the women to go out of the door to a van. So the women went out the door. About five minutes later, the guards began to march us out to the vans. Walking with chains and cuffs on is not easy. If you step too far the cuffs on your ankles really hurt. I was able to manage because years ago, I spent many hours running ropes in football and it prepared me for this. I finally reached the van, which was about forty yards, and it was very difficult getting into the van. I had to step up to get into the van and the eighteen-inch chain attached to my ankles made it very difficult. Now I was sitting in the van and we were headed to court. In court, I was expecting to post bail and get out of jail. Then I would buy a plane ticket and fly to Baton Rouge. Once I was in Baton Rouge, I could find out what was going on. Then I could pay off whatever I need to pay off. Then I could fly back to Utah and be back at work on Friday, maybe Monday at the latest. This seemed like a pretty good deal. I could put up with this craziness for one day.

We arrived at the courthouse in Provo and parked at some type of back entry. There was a metal gate that opened to allow the van to enter. Then the metal gate closed after the van entered. The guard had us get out of the van and stand in front of the back door to the courthouse building. The door opened and we entered the building. The guards took us to a holding room. This was a cement rectangular room maybe 20x40 with a small, open toilet. There was a bench along three sides of the walls. The door to this room was a metal door with a small, four-inch square, peep window. The guards took us into this room. The women had a similar room where they stayed. The holding room for men could hold maybe 30 people. We sat in this room for about 30 minutes. There were wife beaters, drunks, robbers, drug users, child support offenders, drug dealers, illegal aliens, hit and run drivers, and men who had committed many other types of crime in the room. Then there were the murderers and child molesters and others brought in later. This was not a good feeling, but I was only minutes from seeing a judge and getting out of jail.

Finally, the guards called a group of us to go into a courtroom. We got into the elevator to go upstairs where the courtrooms were located. There were about 20 of us. We entered the courtroom and sat in the area where the jury would sit during a trial. I was so glad to be there because now I would meet the judge. I could post bail and get out of this jail. I could get the details as to why I was in jail in the first place. There were a number of cases before mine. There was a case with a lady who had a phobia about being in close quarters. She cried the whole time. I believe this woman would die if they left her in a jail cell too long. She was picked up on a drug-related incident. The prosecutor wanted the woman to go to jail. This woman was having a nervous breakdown. I prayed to the Lord to intervene in the judge's thoughts to allow the judge to find a way to release this woman. Finally, the judge overruled the prosecutor and told the woman, "You can go home and we will put a GPS system on you." I was so happy for this woman. Throughout the day, a number of people were released with a GPS system. I was sure I would get the same.

Then I heard my name called by a public defender. I motioned to him and he came to talk to me. He asked me, "Why are you here?" I said, "I was not sure. It seems I have a bad check in Louisiana." The public defender said, "Let me check." He left and then came back with a sheet of paper. The paper stated I was charged with larceny and fraud in the state of Louisiana. I told the public defender that I needed a GPS and I would fly to Louisiana to correct this issue. He told me that this would not be possible. He said I would have to stay in jail until the state of Louisiana picked me up. I asked him, "How long will that take"? He stated, "It could be up to 6 weeks." I thought you have got to me kidding. He asked me to sign the paper and not appeal this ruling. I told him I would not sign the papers. He said I could come back to court the next day and try something else. He said he did not know of any legal way I could get out of this. "Wow! This would destroy everything I had put together in Utah." I would lose everything if I were in jail for six weeks.

I waited for others to have their court time. I decided to not sign the paper and try to contact people I knew before I committed to signing the paper. Then the judge was told that I did not want to see him but needed time to think. The guard told all of us who had seen the judge, or in my case was not going to see the judge, to leave the courtroom. We all stood and with chains on our legs and handcuffs on our wrists, marched out of the courtroom to the elevator. The elevator led back to the holding room. Now, upon our return, there were over 50 people in the holding room. There was a lot of cursing and very bad language. The room became very bad smelling quickly. There was only one toilet and it was stopped up. This was not a good place to be. We stayed there for over an hour. It was infested with human smells. It was sickening. This was not a place for the weak at heart or the strong at heart either.

The guards finally came to take us back to the jail. So we lined up and the guards made sure that all of us were present and accounted for. The women went out first and then the men. By this time my ankles had swollen and the cuffs were too tight. It was very painful to walk. But I would not seek help or speak with the guards. I just took the pain and waddled to the bus. I was so down after finding out I would be in jail for an unknown amount of time. How could this be?

We made it back to the jail complex and the cuffs were removed. I went to my jail cell and put on the medical socks I had to wear to reduce the swelling of my ankles. I was sitting here in jail trying to figure a way out of this place. I called Debbie to give her the results of my court visit. Debbie was so disappointed to hear that I might be in jail for another six weeks! Let me tell you I was so disappointed myself. I was sure I would not get any sleep that night.

Chapter 4

When I turned eighteen, I had to move out of my parents' house so I went off to college. Now, ironically this is where my biggest religious experience took place. It seemed that no one knew about a secret that I had. I played football and I was a somewhat popular person. I had done many different things, some good some not so good. However, when I was alone with my thoughts, I would sit and wonder about the world and about life. Where did we come from? Where do we go when die? What was life really all about? I wondered most about who was Jesus Christ. I also wondered why God would need a son.

I was sitting in my room one afternoon and I was thinking about my mother. My mother said something I did not understand. She said when she was fifteen years old she was saved. From that point, she then lived her life governed by the teachings of Jesus Christ and the Bible. My mother was close to sixty years old by this time. I thought what if this idea of Christianity is not true. What if someone just made up this concept and over the years, it had become a religion. This would mean that she had wasted her life worshipping a God that did not exist. This touched my heart so much that I began to wonder what I needed to do to find out if Christianity was true. Somehow, I needed to do something to save my mom if Christianity was not true. When I was registering for my classes in my freshmen year, I saw this class called Religion 101. I thought I should take this class so that I could learn about religions. Therefore, I registered for the religion class. Go figure, me taking a religion class!

I showed up for class on the first day and we had an instructor who was a weird guy. He came in the first day and asked the class, "Um... I want to know what is your definition of religion?" This was his first question on the first day of class! Therefore, someone who was Catholic got up and talked about the Pope, Hail Mary's, and things of that nature. Someone stood and talked about being baptized. Another talked about John the Baptist and other things about their religious beliefs. Another student stood and talked about the Holy Ghost. Still another talked about shouting and crying as what religion meant. The instructor continued around the room. All of these students from different Christian denominations had different things to say about their particular denomination. I could really see that somehow Christianity was different based on the denomination. Then the professor looked at me and asked, "Son, you have not said anything. What do you think is the definition of religion?" I really did not want to say anything. All of my experience with discussing religion had been negative. However, who cares, how can I learn without participating? I told the class, "You know I am not sure about Christianity. Because I know there are people around the world who do not know about Jesus Christ. These people do not know about the ideas that we have. I think they have different ideas. I would like to know what their ideas are concerning life and what is going on in this world." The class listened to me and did not say anything. Then the professor just said, "Oh, son, you are going to love this class." Then he went on and said to the whole class, "Ok, today I am going to give you all the definition of religion." He said, "Just imagine a cave man! He comes out of his cave and sees an elephant. The elephant begins to knock over the cave man's garden. The cave men runs out to stop the elephant. He throws his spear and the spear did not stop the elephant. Then the cave man watches the elephant run over and kill another cave man.

The cave man knows immediately that the elephant is greater than he. Therefore, the cave man begins to worship the elephant. Then one day the cave man finds out that the elephant can die. When he sees the dead elephant, he knows that he doesn't need to worship the elephant anymore. So then, a storm comes and the cave man goes out with his spear to stop the storm and he throws his spear into the wind and the wind blows his hut down. In addition, the man thought wow that wind is much more powerful than I am! Therefore, man began to worship the wind. Then later on when fire was discovered, the man saw fire on the ground and man stuck his hand into it and man said oh this burns! Then the man began to worship fire. Man began to worship anything that was greater than he. Therefore, when he looked up in the sky and saw the moon he said the moon is greater than I am so I am going to worship the moon. Then when the rain came, the man knew that he could not control the rain so man began to worship the rain. What began to happen is that man began to have many gods. The god of wind, the god of fire, the god of the sun, and he begin to seek ways to worship these gods. So the definition of religion is man's attempt to relate to a power that is greater than he."

When that Professor said that I immediately knew what religion was! It was not Jesus Christ. It was not God. It was just us trying to relate to powers greater than us. Yet I believed at that time that there was a power that ran the universe and that knowing what that power was was the key to religion. I began to seek out this power. I wanted to know, "Who controls the power that controls the universe?" Whoever controls that power is what these people are calling God. Therefore, I began to think the only way I could find out what that power was would be to study all of the religions of the world. I needed to find out what religion the people around the world believed in. I could not limit my study to just what the people in the United States believed. I knew I could not just focus on Christianity and Jesus Christ. I knew I must study what other people believed. I felt that there was a correlation between the religions of the world. I felt that when I found that correlation, I would be able to communicate with the power that controlled the universe.

Immediately my thoughts had gone way over board and I began to seek out some answers to these questions. I felt I would start out by studying Christianity because my mother was a Christian and I might as well start there. The only thing I knew to do to understand Christianity was to take the Bible and start at page one. I began to read and study the Bible and I read it all the way from Genesis through Revelations. I read the whole Bible. When I finished I remember sitting in my room thinking that it was interesting. All of the stories in the Bible were interesting and that was great. However, I really did not understand what was so great about the book. I really did not understand why Christians believed this stuff. I really did not get the heart of the Bible. I did not find what I was looking for in the Bible.

Therefore, what I decided to do next was to gain an understanding of the difference between all of the Christian denominations. I began to study the Catholic faith, and then Presbyterian, Baptist, and Pentecostal faiths, as well as other denominations. I went through as many denominations as I could and kept studying them. What I noticed was one pattern about all denominations. Surprisingly, all of the denominations believed the same thing about Jesus Christ being the Son of God. They all believed that a long time ago, God made the earth. Then God made all of the people on the earth. The people of these Christian denominations were all trying to serve God in some kind of way. There was a belief that if you served God well, He would acknowledge us and bring us to this place called Heaven. This seemed to be the central point of this whole concept of this Christianity. The more I studied the more I did not believe it. It just did not make sense to me, but I understood what all these denominations were trying to accomplish. The people who were Christians wanted to relate to this God. This God had a son named Jesus Christ. By relating to God via Jesus Christ, God might choose you, after you die, to live in this place called Heaven. This was a very bizarre concept to me.

As I continued to go through all of these Christian denominations, I began to notice something else. All of these denominations in reality were the same, but they all thought they were different. In my opinion, they were all trying to accomplish the same thing, but were going about this in different ways. That was confusing to me because I could not understand the logic of how you could be different, but have only one manual and that manual was the Bible. I felt since everyone believed the Bible, how could one denomination be different from another. That just did not make sense to me at all. Not at all! While I was studying Christianity I begin to wonder, how did black people become Christians anyway?

Blacks were born in Africa and were brought to America as slaves! In addition, we were not Christians when we were in Africa. We were something else! I do not know what religion we were. However, we came to America and the people that brought us to America made us slaves. They killed us, they impregnated our women, and they treated us as if we were animals. These people called themselves Christians. With the way the Christians treated Blacks, why would any black person want to be a Christian? However, the truth of the matter was most black people were Christians because their slave owners were Christians. When the black people were freed, the only thing you could be was a Christian. Why would I worship a God that my slave master used against me to make me a slave and oppress me? I was just very confused by this concept.

When I would go out among the different denominations, I would ask the different ministers, "Why are you Baptist?" These ministers would say, "I am Baptist because this is the religion of Jesus Christ." I thought no, no, no, really you do not even know why you are a Baptist! Let me tell you why. You are Baptist because the slave owner who owned you made you become Baptist. That is why you are a Baptist! That is why you are a Christian! That is why you are all these things! Therefore, I rejected the whole concept of Christianity. I rejected the whole concept of Jesus Christ. I rejected all of these things. I just did not want anything to do with it. I knew that I needed to study it more before I could talk to my mom and explain what I had learned through my research.

The other thing that I discovered was that all of the Christian denominations were spinoffs of the Catholic Church. Now this did not make any logical sense to me at all. The Romans were the people that killed Jesus Christ. They used the Christian religion for their purposes and in turn spread it all over the world. They advanced the concept of Christianity through their military crusades around the world. The Romans would conquer a country then forced the people to be Christians against their will. How could the Romans be considered a righteous people? This was not logical to me. The Romans could not be a righteous people! However, history supported the notion that the Roman Catholic Church was established this way. Then, Martin Luther got upset with the Catholic Church and broke off from the Catholic Church. The people who broke off from the Catholic Church would create their own church and call it the Lutheran Church. Then, after the Lutheran Church, other churches were formed: the Baptist, Methodist, and other churches. These churches were spinoffs of the Catholic Church that could not be Jesus' Church in the first place! How was it possible that if the Catholic Church could not be Jesus' Church, that any of the churches that spun off from the Catholic Church could be the true Church of Jesus Christ? So now, I was very confused. I was a nineteen-year-old boy who was totally lost and had no concept as to why anyone would believe this idea of Christianity.

I continued to study the different denominations. I remember one day out of shear frustration, after six to eight months, maybe even a year of studying the different denominations I came to a conclusion.

I was sitting in my dorm room and there were two more denominations that I needed to go through because I had been through all of the rest of them. One of those two was called the Jehovah Witnesses. Now I knew about them already. I had studied them before. In addition, I did not have any belief in them anyway so I really did not want to study them again. Then there was the last one on the list. It was called The Church of Jesus Christ to Latter Day Saints. Now I had never really heard of them before, but the name was The Church of Jesus Christ. Therefore, I immediately knew that there was no reason for me to study that church. I just could not take it... I just could not stomach any more garbage about this Jesus Christ character. In my opinion, all of these ideas were completely ridiculous. Therefore, as I sat there in my room I thought, well... What can I do? It just does not seem that Christianity can be true. However, I remember my mom having this belief that if you pray to God, He would respond to you. Now I believed everything my mom said and that is what she told me. Therefore, I was sitting in my room that day and I thought you know what? The only person who could possibly comprehend this massive mess that we call Christianity would be the person who created it in the first place. If it was created by the God that they were talking about, then I needed to go talk to Him. The only way I knew to talk to Him was to pray; and that was all I knew.

Therefore, I left my dorm room that day and I ran across the campus. The distance across campus was probably a half mile. I went to a row of trees I knew about. I thought if I could go to the row of trees, I would be closer to nature. My thinking was this would be closer to God. I believed I could call on this God and He would speak to me. There was never a doubt in my mind that He would speak to me. My mom said so. I knew that God was going to speak to me because I wanted to know the answer to this Christianity concept. I knew that God was the only one who could answer my question. Therefore, I was standing there, it must have been one hundred degrees, the sun was shining and the sky was about as blue as could be. I was standing there right at the edge of the row of trees. I said, "God, if Jesus Christ is your son and Christianity is the religion we are supposed to believe, then I need for You to talk to me and let me know that this is true." Really, I did not know what else to ask, so I asked, "Well… okay, God, could you do a miracle for me? There is not a cloud in the sky and the sun is shining. Could you make a bolt of lightning strike out of the sky right now for me? If you do that, I will believe that Christianity is true." And I looked in the sky and I waited. And there was no bolt of lightning. I could not believe it. Because I knew there was going to be a strong bolt of lightning because I believed my mom. I did not believe in God, but I did believe my mom. My mom knew what she was talking about. So then, I was looking at this limb in the tree. And I said, "God, if Christianity is true could you make that limb that I am looking at fall out of the tree? And I'll believe that Christianity is true." And I waited. And the limb did not fall. Now I was getting a little concerned that something was not right. Because how was it possible that this powerful God that these people worshipped couldn't even make a limb fall out of the tree. I was worried for my mom because she believed this idea. So then, I thought I would give Him something easier to do. I was looking at the leaves in the tree and I was looking at one particular leaf. I said, "God, if you are God and you have a son named Jesus Christ and we are supposed to be Christians, all I want you to do is make that one particular leaf fall off the tree and I will believe." And I waited. And the leaf did not fall. All of a sudden, this overwhelming feeling came over me. Tears began to run down my face. I felt that this was the pain of knowing that what my mom had spent her whole life believing was wrong. As I stood there I said, "This God of the Bible is not true. There is no Jesus Christ. And all of this stuff has been made up by man to deceive the people into giving them money or something. But I am finished with Christianity and I will never be a Christian." I remember leaving that field that day and I went back to my dorm room. I took all of the Christian books and materials I had studied and packed them in a box. I decided that I was going to study the religions of the world. I was finished with

Christianity. I was finished with Jesus Christ. I was finished with the God of the Bible. It was over. Now I needed to find a way to go home and tell my mom.

Chapter 5

Day 3

This had been a very long night. I knew now that I was not getting out of this situation easily. I was going to be in jail for a while. The thing that bothered me the most was that I didn't know why. It was 4:45 am and I was awake trying to find some hope. Can you imagine what it would be like to be locked up in jail and not even know why? The day started about the same, I was locked up and found myself praying to the Lord for help. Everything in me was being tested now. I began to do, what I always did when things were not going right in my life, I turned inward to strengthen myself. But this time there was something different. I knew I was not alone. I knew that my brother, Jesus Christ, was with me. I knew that my Father in Heaven was with me. I knew that they would help me, but not save me. They would not come to this jail and remove me from it. What they would do was strengthen me in my time of need. This was my greatest trial since I accepted Jesus Christ as my Lord and Savior.

Now I heard the sound from the guards, "Get up and stand at the door of your cell for the count." Every morning there was a shift change for the guards. The new guard had to come around and count the prisoners to confirm that we were all there. Then prisoners were allowed to leave their cells to take certain medications if they were needed. The guards would allow about ten prisoners from their cell at a time to come and take their "meds". Then those ten prisoners would go back to their cell and another ten would be allowed out of their cell. I will try to describe how the cells were setup. The complete bay is about thirty yards by thirty yards. You enter into the bay from a hallway. There is a locked glass door that allowed you entry into the bay. The bay is setup with about ten tables with each table having built-in benches. The complete table system would allow about forty prisoners to sit at one time. There is a TV area, which can seat about twenty people. Then along the back wall are the prisoner's cells, about forty on the bottom and forty on top or upstairs. Each cell is about six feet wide and twelve feet long. At the front of the room is a commode. About three feet from the commode is a set of bunk beds. There is no privacy at all. The door to the cell has a glass front about six inches wide and five feet long. This glass is used by the guards to make sure nothing strange is going on in the cells. Each cell holds two prisoners. These doors stay locked.

The prisoners finished taking their meds. The guards opened the doors for us to come out and get our breakfast. The bottom cells got their food first. Then the prisoners in the top cells were allowed out to get their food. I stayed in the top cells. The food was taken back to our rooms for us to eat. The food was okay. I gave most of it away. My cellmate was a Hispanic. He was in jail for not showing up at court for traffic violations. We finished eating and were allowed out of our cells to take the trays downstairs. Then we went back to our cells to clean up. When we finished cleaning our cells, the guard would lock us up. We had to wait in our cell for the time when the guards would let us out to go into the open bay. Waiting in the cell was a very difficult thing. You couldn't go anywhere. You were trapped like an animal. You had to have very good control of your mind to handle this situation. I was sitting there waiting for two hours so that I could get out of this cell to call Debbie. My heart was heavy. My mind was racing at a thousand miles a second trying to figure out how I could get out of here before I lost everything! I was losing my job, my house, and there was nothing I could do. I was waiting to get out of this cell so that I could call Debbie. Debbie was my only source to the outside world and I needed her to help me. Somehow, Debbie would have to find out why I was in jail. Then we could work on what had to be done for me to get out of here. Finally, we were allowed out of our cell. I went over to the phone and called Debbie. There was no answer. Oh God, let her be safe. Debbie was supposed to get her driver's license today. My mind began to wonder all sorts of things. Did the city of Baton Rouge have a warrant for Debbie also? Had the police picked her up and taken her to jail? The pain of these thoughts was so great, that my heart cried out, "Lord, do not let anything happen to her." Three more times I called Debbie and there was no answer. Now it was time to go back into lockup. I began to constantly plea with God to protect Debbie and help her get through another day. The Lord assured me that Debbie was okay. I knew how to identify the Holy Ghost. What a wonderful gift to have. The Holy Ghost spoke to my heart and set me at peace.

Back in my cell now, I tried to take a nap, but sleep would not come. I begin reading the Bible; it comforted me and gave me hope. I was sitting there waiting to call Debbie. I knew it would be about four hours before I could call her. I had been reading the Bible for about two hours. The guard stated, "It's lunch time." I knew it would not be long before I could call Debbie. Finally, lunch was over. I was getting closer to being able to call Debbie. Two more hours in the cell and the guard allowed us to leave the cell. I was now out of the cell and could call Debbie. I made my way to the phone and called her. Two rings and she answered. My heart was overjoyed to hear her voice. Debbie was okay. The Lord had answered my prayer. I wanted to cry, but I could not. You see my surroundings would not allow these type things. I was happy because Debbie was the love of my life. I truly enjoyed talking with Debbie. Still neither she nor I had the answer as to why I was in jail. I finished talking to Debbie. Our time out of the cell was very close to being over as I began to look for another copy of the Bible. The NIT version that I had been reading had taken out the feelings of the words of the Bible. I needed to find the King James version of the Bible so that I could feel the words of the scriptures. I found one!

Now I was back in lockup. I was reading the Old Testament. I felt the need to pray for help. I pleaded with the Lord via prayer. "Father, show me a way out of this trial." "Father what do I need to do?" The Lord was silent. No words. Then the Lord spoke to my mind and these are the words that He said, "Send a payment of $88.00 to the bank. Send payments of $100 to the other accounts. Tell Larry to plead my case before the court. You can post bail via Larry." I really needed to save my job. If I was transported to Louisiana, I would lose everything. "Larry is to ask the court to set a court date and I will fly to Baton Rouge. Send $40 to the court system to pay court fees. Offer to pay more via Larry." The Lord spoke these words to my mind. Then the time came that I could call Debbie again. I called Debbie and told her all that the Lord had said to me. Now I waited in peace for Debbie to carry out these things. My mind was clear. My heart was at peace. I did not mind going back to my cell for the night. I continued to read the Old Testament as the Spirit continued to open my mind to the understanding of the scriptures. I suddenly realized something, "I don't want to be here, yet I have had two very good missionary experiences."

When I was in the first holding cell, I was asked by some of the guys, "What religion are you?" I told them that I was a member of the Church of Jesus Christ of Latter Day Saints. One of them asked me, "Are you really a Mormon?"

I said, "That is what the members of the church are called."

The young man stated, "I used to be a member of that church but I am not any longer."

I asked, "So what happened that caused you to no longer be a member?"

He said I am not sure, I just could not believe that Joseph Smith was a prophet.

I asked him, "Why is it so hard to believe that Joseph was a prophet?"

He said, "Because Joseph Smith did some bad things in his life."

He went on to tell me some of the things that Joseph had done. I asked him did he know any of the prophets of the Old Testament. He said he did and named off Moses, David and some others. I showed him in the Old Testament that these prophets had also done bad things in their lives. The young man was surprised to find out that prophets made mistakes and did bad things. Somewhere in his mind, a prophet was perfect. Once he understood that prophets were men and made the same mistakes as other man, he said, "I must go back and study the Church of Jesus Christ of Latter Day Saints again." There was another guy listening. This guy said that he did not know anything about the Church of Jesus Christ of Latter Day Saints. This guy had been picked up for drug trafficking. He was carrying drugs from California to Washington. The police pulled him over for speeding and in a search found the drugs. He asked me, "What is the difference between the Mormon Church and any other Christian church."

I find this to be ironic. Here is a question for your thought. "Why is it that a person who is not a Christian sees the Mormons and the Christian as the same? Yet some Christians will say that the Mormons are not Christians?" I told him they are the same in whom they worship. He asked me then, "Why do Christians dislike Mormons?"

I told him that when the Christians had more information about the gospel of Jesus Christ, the Jews did not like them. The information Christians had created a change in the traditions of the Jews. For this reason, many of the Jews rejected Jesus and his teachings. The same applies today. The Church of Jesus Christ of Latter Day Saints has more information about the gospel of Jesus Christ. The other Christian denominations reject this new information concerning the gospel just as the Jews rejected the Christians. I gave him some scriptures to read. They both were very accepting to the things they heard. I prayed that it would change their lives.

Well, it was time to go to bed. Lights out was at 10:00 pm. This was my first weekend in jail. Well, here we go!

Chapter 6

At this point, I began to do something very unusual. I went to church now all of a sudden. I had a very good friend named Peggy. One day I asked her, "Could I go to church with you some time?" She had asked me many times to go to church with her but I would never even consider it. Going to church was something that did not interest me. I am sure she was shocked but I went to church with her. As we were sitting there in church, the minister started preaching and saying things and everybody was saying, amen, amen, amen! And I was thinking, but why are you all saying amen? What this person is saying is not even true. It is not even in this book that you all call the Bible. I raised my hand and she grabbed my hand and said, "You can't do that." I said, "But he's not telling you all the truth! Because what he's talking about is not even in the Bible. He's just making up things and someone needs to stop him." I did not like these people being misled. I am sure Peggy knew there was something weird about me. Never again did she allow me to go to church with her.

I would go home on the weekend and talk with my sister. We lived in Moss Point, MS at the time. My sister's name is Mary but we called her Nell. She was a very special sister who passed away early in life. I would go home to discuss certain scriptures in the Bible with her. Ironically, I knew the Bible very well, and I would use the scriptures against her. I wanted to find some way to change her mind about Christianity and then she could help me talk to my mom. Together, I felt we could get my mom to understand that the Bible was not true. I would pull the scriptures out and say, "What does this mean?" She would say, "Well I'm not sure what that means." I would always pull out the scriptures that the preachers and ministers never talked about. Because I knew that people did not read the Bible, they just did whatever the minister said. I really felt that church was a big racket that preachers used to earn a living. For years, I would talk with Nell to try to get her on my side. At this time in my life, I did not even believe that Jesus Christ ever existed. I went into that line of trees and called on him and He did not show up. Now I decided to seek out the super power that controls this world that people call God or Jesus Christ.

Therefore, I began studying different religions of the world. Let me tell you, it is going to be hard to believe this, but over the next three years, I studied Buddhism, Zoroastrianism, Hinduism, Jainism, Sikhism, and many other religions. There were so many religions that I cannot even think of all of them anymore. I studied every religion that I could get my hands on from everywhere in the world. Then I began to realize that there were many different people all over the world that did not believe, and in some cases had not even heard of Christianity. They had never heard of Jesus Christ. They had never heard of these Christian things that we hold so dear. There were billions of people who had never heard of Jesus Christ. I thought that was crazy! Because I remembered a scripture, in the Bible, John 3:1-7, I will paraphrase this scripture. When Nicodemus came to Jesus Christ and said, "I know you are a person who has come from God otherwise you could not do the things which you do." Then Jesus said something real bizarre to Nicodemus, he said, "Unless a man is born again he cannot enter the Kingdom of Heaven." Then Nicodemus asked, "Is it possible for a man to enter his mother's womb a second time, and be born?" Then Jesus says,

"You don't really understand what I'm saying. You've got to be born of water and of the spirit to enter into the Kingdom of Heaven." Now this scripture was very important to me. Jesus said you must be baptized or you cannot enter the Kingdom of God (Heaven).

Now let me digress a bit and tell you about something that happened to me a short while ago. We had a meeting once in college with the local clergies. Ministers of the different denominations came to this one location. I think there were Catholic, Methodist, Pentecostal, Presbyterian, Lutheran, and a couple other religious leaders there. These leaders sat at a table and we as a religion class had the opportunity to ask them any question that we wanted. Some of us had gotten together the night before so we could come up with tough questions so that we could trip these ministers up. I remember that day very well and the different questions that everybody asked. These ministers answered every question asked and everything was going fine. Now in our little group we were radical. We really were. We wanted to stump the Christian leaders. Our questioning started with an attempt to set up the leaders. We wanted to back the leaders into a corner by asking simple questions. Then we had one major question to ask after the set up. We started by asking the ministers, "Is God a good God?" The ministers all answered, "Yes, God is a good God. And God loves us! Yes, He loves us. God gave His only begotten Son to die on the cross for our sins." We did not want such a long answer but it was okay. Our next question, "Is everything in the Bible true?" The ministers again all agreed by saying, "Yes, everything in the Bible is true. The Bible contains all the words of God." At this point, the set up was going as planned. We asked the ministers to open their scriptures to John 3:1-7. We asked them to read the scripture. These were the words of the scripture:

"1 There was a man of the Pharisees, named Nicodemus, a ruler of the Jews:
2 The same came to Jesus by night, and said unto him, Rabbi, we know that thou art a teacher come from God: for no man

can do these miracles that thou doest, except God be with him.

3 Jesus answered and said unto him, Verily, verily, I say unto thee, Except a man be born again, he cannot see the kingdom of God.

4 Nicodemus saith unto him, How can a man be born when he is old? can he enter the second time into his mother's womb, and be born?

5 Jesus answered, Verily, verily, I say unto thee, Except a man be born of water and of the Spirit, he cannot enter into the kingdom of God.

6 That which is born of the flesh is flesh; and that which is born of the Spirit is spirit.

7 Marvel not that I said unto thee, Ye must be born again." (KJV)

We asked the ministers, "Are the words of these scriptures true?" They all agreed, "Yes, every word of the Bible is true." Now the trap was set. It was time to spring the question that we knew the Christian leaders could not answer. However, I felt a couple more questions would seal the deal. We then ask the ministers, "Would God ever betray us?" The ministers all agreed, "No, God will never betray us." Now we asked the ministers, "In the scriptures we read earlier, what does being born of the water mean?" All but one of them stated, "It means being baptized." This one minister said that born of the water means being born from your mother. He stated that when you are born, your mother's water breaks and this is being born of the water. Then we immediately dismissed his concept by stating that he misunderstood just as Nicodemus did. Jesus said you must be born again. Now your idea of the mother's water breaking was correct for the first birth. However, the second birth was not possible for a man cannot reenter his mother and have a second birth. This minister retracted his idea and agreed with the rest of the ministers, that the verse meant being baptized. Another question to the ministers, "So would you all agree that Jesus states a person must be baptized to enter the Kingdom of Heaven?"

All of the ministers agreed, "Yes, you must be baptized to enter the Kingdom of Heaven". One final question and the stage would be set. We asked the ministers, "Where is the Kingdom of Heaven?" Again, they all agreed that this place is the same as Heaven, the place where God lives.

Now everything was set. It was time for the question we spent all of this time setting up. I repeated to the religious leaders what they had agreed to be true. We wanted to make sure there was no misunderstanding. I stated the following,

> "Then all the things that we discussed that appear in the Bible are true, and God is a good God and Jesus died on a cross for our sins, and we need to be baptized and confess that Jesus Christ is our Lord and Savior, and by doing these things we can enter the Kingdom of Heaven."

All of the ministers agreed, "Yes, these things are true. We feel that you all really have a good understanding of these scriptures." Okay, then we asked the panel this question; "There were billions of people who lived before Jesus Christ was born, who were good people and died never hearing of Jesus Christ. In addition, there were billions of people who lived on the earth at the time that Jesus Christ was on earth, who were good people and died never hearing of Jesus Christ. In addition, there are billions of people living on earth today, who are good people, and who will die never hearing of Jesus Christ. They all are nevertheless God's children. These people will never be baptized, because they never heard of Jesus Christ and cannot accept Him. When Jesus states you must be baptized in order to enter into the Kingdom of Heaven, then that would imply that none of those people, who have never heard of Jesus Christ would enter Heaven because they cannot be baptized, because they have already died. So, what is going to happen to them?"

The ministers began to talk among themselves. These ministers began to reason with each other. We kept saying, "No, no, no if the Bible is true then these people cannot enter the Kingdom of Heaven because they are not baptized. If that is not true then Jesus must have lied. Or is the Bible wrong?" We continued to pressure these religious leaders for a response. This went on probably for about five minutes. The ministers just could not give us an answer. Finally, one minister, I think he was Baptist, said, "These other ministers, my colleagues, are not willing to answer your question, but I'm going to answer your question. If you're not baptized, you're going to go to Hell." I remember saying to him, "So what you're telling me, then, is that this good God, who loves us, condemns us if we are born in a location where we will not hear about Jesus Christ? So you are telling me that all these people do not qualify to go to Heaven and so the only other place they can go is Hell?" The minister looked right into my eyes and said, "Yes, that is exactly what I am telling you because that is what the Bible says." That day I said, "Man, there isn't a chance in this world that I'll be a Christian. I will never enter a Christian church again! I will never be a Christian. I do not want anything to do with Jesus Christ or the Bible." I became very bitter. I just continued to study more world religions. I remember studying a religion called Jainism. I really got into this religion. If you get a chance, you should look at it. I will not talk about it in this book.

I began to study the ministers of the Christian religion. I wondered how these ministers could get so many people to believe in their religion. I noticed that the Christian ministers all had a program that they followed. It was a concept of elevating the spirit of the people through music in order to get them excited. When they got the people excited, the people would give more money. I began to notice these different ministers just ripping people off. They were taking the people's money left and right. Then I began to realize that this whole concept of Christianity was a major rip-off and it was a money-making machine. The preachers knew how to play the crowd.

Ministers have some theatrical things that they put on and they would call it preaching. They would dance a little bit and say, "oh God" and "oh Jesus" and they would say these little things and make sounds like "ha" and "yah". This caused people to get more emotional. When the people got emotional, the ministers would say, "Oh, they have the Holy Ghost on them." The people would be caught up in the trick that was being played on them. I watched it from church to church and from minister to minister. It was so disgusting. It came to the point where I disliked Christianity. I just hated the behavior of these preachers and all that they stood for. It was not the gospel I had an issue with, it was how it was being used for personal gain. The whole thing was just so unbelievable.

I was about twenty years old at this time. I began to study Islam. Now Islam was a very interesting religion. They had a God and his name was Allah. Allah was one God. I was intrigued by the concept of one God. Then they had this religious leader named Mohammed. They believed that the angel Gabriel, the same one that came to see Mary to tell her she was pregnant with Jesus Christ, came to see Mohammed. Supposedly, Gabriel told Mohammed that Christianity was not intended to be a religion. People had turned Jesus Christ, who was a great prophet, into something more than he was and created a religion based on His teachings. Mohammad further stated that Jesus Christ had never intended for a religion to be created from the messages He taught. I thought, hmm, that is interesting. Therefore, with these thoughts, I began to study Islam seriously.

Back in the early eighties, it was hard to get an English version of the Quran, the Islamic scriptures, but I got one. I continued to study this book. As I was studying the Quran, I found it to be an interesting book. One day I was reading the Quran and came across some very interesting scriptures. Let me see if I can explain this. In the Quran, Jesus Christ was in heaven and he was talking to Allah. Allah says to Jesus Christ basically, "What is this that you have done on earth?

I did not send you there to create a religion." Jesus said, "No, it was man who created this religion. The people took the teachings that I gave them, from You, and made me the deity." I remember reading that and that passage hit me so powerfully. It hit a sense in my brain that exploded my thinking. Now let me tell you what really happened to me. It was not the story that I just told you, where Jesus and Allah were talking. It was not that the Quran talked about Jesus dying on a cross and being raised from the dead by Allah to show his power. It was not that. This is what it was: I immediately thought of a question that hit me very hard and rocked my soul. This question touched my heart and mind. How it is possible that an Islamic book called the Quran would know of Jesus Christ? No matter what the words in the Quran stated, this is what I heard. "Jesus Christ was born, lived, died, came back to life, and never died again." Now I immediately wrote that down in my mind and in my heart. "Jesus Christ was born, lived, died, came back to life, and never died again and the Quran was a witness of this." Now, needless to say, there was a second witness of what the Quran had just stated, called the Bible. In the New Testament there was a young man born named Jesus. In addition, he lived, and he died, and he came back to life and never died again. Now I had two witnesses, the Bible and the Quran of this Jesus Christ doing the same things. I began to go back through every religion that I had ever studied to try to find if any claimed to have a deity who was born, lived, died, come back to life and did not die again. Now when Muhammad died he was dead. When Buddha died, he was dead. All of these people of all of the religions, when they died, they were dead. None of these religious deities came back to life. It appeared that Jesus Christ was the only one. So all of a sudden, I began to realize that there was something very special about this character, Jesus Christ. In addition, I needed to know more about him.

Chapter 7

Day 4 & Day 5

I **actually slept** well that night. I thanked Jesus for watching over me as I slept. I probably slept because I had been moved from the holding cell to an individual cell. The bad thing about this was that it meant I would be here for a while. I had breakfast and it was halfway decent. My cellmate and I began to talk. He was here because of some traffic violations. He went to court in one county to clear a warrant. Upon clearing that warrant, it was discovered that he had another warrant in another county. The second county arrested him. Since his records were lost in the system, he had been in jail now for ten days. Since he did not have a lawyer, he was unable to get a court date. This was the system. Now I was caught up in the same system. He and I discussed the reason I was in jail. I knew now that I was arrested because of an outstanding warrant in Louisiana. The warrant was issued over a year ago for me not showing up in court. The interesting thing is that I never knew of this court date. The court system attempted to contact me at my former office. I had closed this office over a year ago. The post office does not forward summons, and for this reason I never received it. Yet I was still responsible for not showing up at court. So the reason I was in jail was because I did not show up for court!

My lawyer in Baton Rouge had founded out that there was a balance due at my bank on one of my business accounts. However, this was all that my lawyer had found out at this time. My lawyer would try to get more information on Monday. Therefore, this was where things stood as of Friday. I was feeling better about things and could hardly wait for Monday. The rest of the day went fine. We were out of the cell for more hours this day. I had a chance to meet many of the other guys. Most of them were here because of drugs, either drug use or trafficking. The interesting thing was that these were some very good kids from some very good families. These guys had wives and kids. They got involved with drugs at an early age and could not break the habit. They had good jobs and their families had no idea that they had these issues.

As the day went on, dinner was served. Now it was time to go back into lockdown. I was lying in my bed now trying to pass the time before I could call Debbie. The guard had a set time when we could make phone calls. For at least one hour, I pleaded with the Lord that I not be taken back to Louisiana. I really needed a way to get out of this problem without losing everything Debbie and I had built in our new life here in Utah. My best chance was for my lawyer to be able to get me bail so I could be at work on Friday. I had promised the Lord all that I had and all that I could give if He would answer my prayer. "Oh God, please help me!" I knew of no one else that could help me. Here was a vision that came to my mind: "On Wednesday, I was called to go to court. In court the judge stated, 'Your warrant has been dropped and you are free to go.'" Oh God, let this vision be true. I really did not want to go back to Louisiana. In the vision, I went home and called every creditor I knew and made arrangement to pay them. Another vision opened to my mind. There was a man in a baker's hat that said to me, "Worry less about money and more about the Kingdom of God. The money will come." I am not sure what this vision meant, but I would study it more. In another vision, I saw the clouds open and a light shining through the cloud. A voice spoke and said, "You wanted to see me?" However,

I saw nothing and the voice said, "You will be out of jail on Thursday. Peace be with you." I tried to hold the vision, but I could not. Then the voice said, "Tell no one what you saw at this time." Then the vision was gone. There was more to this vision then what I will write here. I found this vision to be very interesting. You see, I had always felt that I could see Jesus Christ. I knew that with the proper faith and will of the heart Jesus would appear to me. In this vision, I think Jesus wanted me to focus more on believing without seeing. There was another vision, "I am in the court room. There was a lady in the courtroom. She looked like she was in her late 20s or maybe early 30s. I could see her among everyone else because she had a glow about her. She looked familiar. Tears were beginning to come to my eyes because I thought I knew her. In the vision, she said she was my mother. I asked her, "Why do you say that? My mom has been dead over 10 years." The lady began to tell me things that only she (my mom and I) would know. I knew now that she was my mother in her glory. She was beautiful. Yet I have never seen a picture of my mom when she was young. I saw her in this vision. There was more to this vision. Yet this is all I will write about the vision.

Finally, we were let out of our cells to make phone calls. When my cell opened, I rushed over to the phone to call Debbie. I spoke to Debbie and she was doing well. This was not an easy time for her. Yet I prayed for her to be strong during this time of trouble. I then called my supervisor from work. He and I discussed my situation. It was decided that I had built up enough vacation time to last until the next Thursday. If I was still in jail on that Thursday, I would resign and have Debbie turn in my laptop. I was losing money for every day that passed. The CPA firm where I worked as a consultant was okay because I had already taken off two months.

Now it was time to go back to lockup. My cellmate had seen me reading the Bible. He asked me, "What church do you attend?" I told him I belonged to the Church of Jesus Christ of Latter Day Saints. He then said to me that he joined the same church years ago. He said he never understood the church. He had listened to his friends from other churches attack the LDS Church and he left the church. I asked him, had he joined any other church. He told me he had not. I asked him if he believed there was a God. He told me that he was not sure if there was a God. I knew then where to start when talking to him. I had been in his position before. I knew what he was feeling. Here is the story I told him.

"We live on a planet that is called earth. This earth is round like a ball. There are people who live on top, on the sides and under this ball. The people on the sides and bottom of the earth spend their days driving on streets and highways. As of today, none of them has fallen off the earth. There is water on all sides of the earth in oceans, seas and rivers. None of the water has fallen off the earth. While we do all our daily activities on this round ball, the earth is spinning around at thousands of miles an hour and no one feels it. While we are driving, walking and living our lives, this earth is flying through space around the sun at over 60,000 miles per hour. Yet none of us even notices. There are other planets travelling around the sun. Somehow, none of these planets runs into each other. Then the sun is a mass of continuous explosions, yet the sun never explodes to the point that it destroys itself. Now I ask you, which is more believable, what I told you about the earth or that there is a God?" His answer was the best answer I have heard from people who I have told this story. He stated, "There would have to be a God, otherwise the whole concept you explain about the earth could not work." I told him that he was right. Surely, there must be a God. He agreed. Then he asked me, "Why are you not trying to get me to join your church?" I told him, "Sometimes a person is not ready to understand more than they can comprehend." I asked him to think about the things that I told him that night. Then if something in you says I want to know more, you will ask me. I told him to know this, "Religion is man's attempt to relate to the God we talked about tonight." I could tell he was thinking about the things that I said. Now it was time for the Holy Ghost to speak to him and give him a desire to want to know more. It was time for lights out. I went to bed.

Day 5

I slept very well last night. I thanked the Lord for allowing me to see this Sabbath day. I am very tired today. I ate breakfast and cleaned my cell. Then I went back to sleep. The Lord had brought comfort to my soul. I covenanted with the Lord to:

- Attend the temple twice a month.
- Show more affection to Debbie
- Find all debts and setup payments to pay them
- To have a closer relationship with my sisters and brothers
- To have a closer relationship with my children and grandchildren
- To do genealogy work for my family and others

I would be at work on Friday, October 5th at Property Solutions. I sealed this covenant with my heart and soul between my Heavenly Father and myself. Amen..

I called to talk to Debbie. She was holding up okay. Her hope was tied to, "And this too shall pass." She was a strong woman but she was alone. I was here in jail while A.J. was serving his mission for the Lord in Richmond, VA. I prayed to Heavenly Father that He would give Debbie strength and let the members of the church help her until I was able to get there on Thursday. Here in jail, we were allowed to send emails. But this was the second day that emails would not work. I left the email machine for a few minutes. I went back later and the machine was working. I sent Debbie two emails. These emails gave Debbie more instructions about what to do on Monday.

Back in my cell, I read the Old Testament. I was at the point where Moses took Israel and left Egypt. I had just finished reading the last couple of day's writings. I was writing about this experience of being in jail. How glorious the Lord has been to me. About two weeks ago, I began to prepare myself to see Jesus Christ in the flesh. In a vision

Jesus gave me, I did not see Him, but He spoke to me. I couldn't share this information yet. I prayed that He would allow me to share this information in the future.

I went to church today. I did not know this but they have church meetings here in jail. It was great. I could not stop crying. The Spirit was so high today. I had to wipe tears from my eyes often, for the Spirit of the Lord was upon me. The subject today was "Love." The teacher did a great job. I knew that Debbie was at Church at the same time I was. I was so glad to be a member of the Church of Jesus Christ of Latter Day Saints.

Now that I was back from church, my cellmate had so many questions. My cellmate told me that he became a Mormon at the age of fifteen. He said the missionaries taught his mother and she joined the LDS church. He said he went to all of the youth functions but never really understood the church. He asked me if it was okay if he asked me questions. I told him he could ask me anything he wanted. He did not say much more and went on with his day. Break time was in about an hour and they were giving us an extra thirty minutes. "Thank you, Jesus!"

I called Debbie. She was not having an easy time. She was moving too slow to get me out of here. I had to stay on her. Debbie was my only hope and she was being much too passive. I asked the Lord to please bless Debbie so that she would find some fire in her heart to make her act. I gave Debbie all the instructions I could think of to work on getting me out of jail. We really had to work hard tomorrow. It was time to go to bed. I was pleading with the Lord with all my heart. I am now reading over my covenants to burn it into my heart. Tomorrow was Monday and I hoped that something would change. Maybe, I would be called to court tomorrow. Maybe, I would have a better idea why I was here. Then I could find a way to get out of here. It was time for lights out and time to try to get some sleep. Good night.

Chapter 8

I **went back** to the Bible. I had decided that I needed to study the Bible a second time. I was not going to study the denominations this time, but only the Bible itself. I had decided to take a different approach. That approach was to understand what the Bible really said, not what the denominations said. I went back to my dorm room because it was time for me to go to work again. I was in search of Jesus Christ to find out why He was so special. When I got to my dorm, I began to put together a journal. I went back to page one of Genesis. I started there to try to understand why Jesus Christ was born, lived, died, came back to life and did not die again. I began to focus on studying the Bible. I began to put my journal together. I tried to link Jesus Christ to everything in the Bible. I wanted to link him to the Old Testament. Most Christians do not believe that Jesus existed in the Old Testament. They believe that only God, the Father, is in the Old Testament. They believe the Israelites followed God, the Father, not Jesus. Most people believe that Jesus did not exist until he was born.

As I began to go through the scriptures again, I diligently studied the scriptures from cover to cover more intently than before. It took a little while, about five to six months of painstaking study to complete the reading of the Bible. I wanted to make absolutely sure that I did not miss anything. When I completed my study of the Bible, I decided that I was still unsure about Christianity. Nevertheless, I was sure about Jesus Christ, and that there was something different about Him. I may have been twenty years old at this time. I do remember when I finished the Bible I still did not believe it. On this day, a question came to my mind, "What would make the Bible true?" I then begin to speak aloud and these are the words I spoke, "There is something wrong with this book. It contradicts itself. Yet it is possible that it could be true, but there are a few flaws in the book." I began to write down questions that I needed answered. "If I could get these questions answered then maybe I can believe in Christianity." You must understand I wanted so badly for the Bible to be true.

I wrote down these six questions. The first question was, "How do you identify the Holy Ghost?" You see, I had attended many churches. In those churches, the way the Holy Ghost was identified was in direct contradiction to the Bible. If you went to the Pentecostal church, they would say that in order for you to have the Holy Ghost you would need to speak in tongues. If you did not speak in tongues, then you did not have the Holy Ghost. Their definition of speaking in tongues was that there was a unique language that you would speak and God would understand the language. No one else could understand this language. The problem was that this concept did not appear in the Bible. So where did they get this concept from? I remember going to the Pentecostal church and asking the preacher, "Where in the Bible is this concept of speaking of tongues that you use to identify the Holy Ghost?" The preacher would take me to Acts and show me where on the day of Pentecost the disciples began to speak in a tongue that was not native to them. I read that scripture many times and I thought, "but that's not what the scripture says." You see the language that the Hebrews spoke was Hebrew, but there were people there in this area that were not Hebrew, and they spoke different languages and the language that they heard was their own language. This was not some language that only God understood. I thought the whole concept was wrong. So how in the world were you supposed to identify what the Holy Ghost was? If you went to the Baptist church they would say,

"Well, in order for you to have the Holy Ghost upon you, you would suddenly feel the urge to stand up, and you would jump up and start dancing, shouting, and sweating, and then you might pass out." I asked, "Where in the Bible did you get this information?" I believed that the Holy Ghost was upon the disciples many times, and I didn't remember any record or story in the Bible where they danced. Not once. I didn't understand where people came up with the Holy Ghost concept. These churches could at least do a better job of imitating the things that were in the Bible.

I began to realize something very interesting. I began to realize that the ministers did not understand the Bible. I formulated the second question. When Moses left Egypt with the Israelites and went out into the desert, why did he build something called a mobile tabernacle? This tabernacle was very similar to a temple. I could not understand why it was so important to build this thing before finding water. Nevertheless, the tabernacle/temple had to be built in order for God to dwell with the people. It made sense that he wanted to dwell with the people. Later on, Solomon actually built a temple. The temple was a place where Jesus Christ spent a lot of his time. If the temple was so important, then why were there no temples today and why did no one even talk about one? Where was the temple? None of these denominations had a temple. What did people do in the temple? So my question was, "Where is your temple or when are you going to build one if you don't have one? And what is the importance of it?"

The next question I had was about the idea of the trinity. I studied the trinity and the trinity concept developed by Constantine was not correct. Constantine was the leader of Rome and his concept carried into the Roman Catholic Church. Constantine's idea was that no man on earth could be greater than him or Caesar. Now understand that Jesus lived on earth. Therefore, the idea was that Christians believed that Jesus was the Son of God, which would make Jesus a God. The Jews believed that Jesus was a prophet but not the Son of

God. The Jews believe that there was only one God. The Jews felt that if someone were the Son of God then there would be two Gods. Then there was this idea of the Holy Ghost, which made things even more confusing. In the meeting at Nicaea, Constantine wanted to bring the Roman Empire under Christianity. The reason he wanted to do that was that he noticed that the Christians would die for what they believed. The Jews would not die for what they believed. Constantine knew that if he could build an army that would die for what they believed, as the Christians would, then he could build a very powerful army. Constantine attempted to instill this concept into the Roman people. Not a concept of Jesus, but the concept of being willing to die for what you believe. He began to turn his kingdom into a Christian kingdom. The problem was that the Jews and Christians kept fighting among themselves. Therefore, Constantine put together this meeting at Nicaea to bring the Christians, Jews and Romans under control. Constantine became the high priest of the Christian religion by appointing himself its leader. Constantine installed a concept that would allow Jesus Christ to be the Son of God, both a man on earth and a God in Heaven. This concept would eliminate the conflict of Jesus being greater than Constantine while Jesus was on earth. The concept worked just great for Rome.

Now my problem was that most Christian denominations did not even understand this concept. A new concept was created that Jesus and God were the same person. For me, there was no way this could be true because Jesus and God could not be the same person. That was what the Christian religion was teaching. However, they were not the same. They were two different people in the Bible. So either God was the Father and Jesus the son (separate beings), or the Bible was wrong. That was my third question: "Why do we make Jesus Christ and God the same person and fall back on the word Trinity?"

The fourth question was that I noticed throughout the whole history of the Bible there were prophets who spoke with God. This prophet would tell the people how God wanted them to live. Therefore, if God was the same today as he was in the past, and was going to be forever, then where was the prophet. Therefore, I wrote that down. If there were a true Christian church, then that church would have a prophet.

My fifth question came from the following idea. While reading the scriptures I noticed that Jesus went about doing good things. He would heal the sick. He would heal broken legs and leprosy. Whatever people were afflicted with, He would simply heal them. Never once did Jesus charge people to be healed. When a man asked, "Jesus, can you heal my arm?" Jesus didn't respond, "I will heal your arm for four hundred dollars." Jesus also never charged people to preach to them. Therefore, I wrote down that if there was a true Christian church then that church would not charge for preaching the word of God, because if you were called by God to preach then He would give the gospel to you freely. If He gave the gospel to you freely, then why would someone pay to be preached to?

The last question I had was based on the idea that if this God was the God of the world, then how could He condemn a person just because of where the person was born? If a person was born in a country where the gospel of Jesus Christ was not taught, how could it be that person's fault for not accepting Jesus Christ as his Savior? However, there were billions of people in many countries in that situation. Should not Heavenly Father put into place a way for these people to enter heaven? However, these people would never be baptized because they were born where Christianity was not the religion of the land. Now these people were condemned to go to hell. The merciful God of the Bible would have some system that would allow these people to be saved or He could not be God. What was this system?

I wrote down, from the whole summation of the Bible, those questions. I took those six questions and I began to seek out who could answer the questions. I would go to different churches and I would ask these questions to many people. In twenty years, I had not asked more than one question because no one had been able to answer any of the questions.

Chapter 9

Day 6 & Day 7

I had gotten very little sleep that night. It was very difficult to sleep when you had no concept of your future and every hour you lost more of what you had. The guard came over the speaker. "Get up and stand by your door." I got out of bed and stood by the door. The new guard went from door to door counting all of the inmates. He counted us and we got back into bed. It was 5:30 and the guard was making the call for everyone who was going to court that day. My name was not called. What a bad feeling to know that there was no chance I would get out of jail that day. We ate breakfast and cleaned up the cell. I would try to go to sleep now since I did not get any sleep that night. I was in bed but sleep escaped me. I began to pray again. "Bless, Debbie, Father." Finally, I fell asleep. I slept about an hour. I pleaded with the Lord the whole time. "Lord, please let me go home and be at work on Friday." I cried to the Lord so much that my heart began to cry out on its own. The Lord showed me a vision that I would give a talk concerning my ordeal. I promised the Lord that I would do it. I stared out the cell door. I felt the Holy Ghost leaving me so I could think as a man. He strengthened me as He left me.

I began reading more in Exodus. I remembered more details of a vision I had last night. I remembered saying, "Glory to God in the

Highest." I spoke these words in the vision. Now I said them outside of the vision. I was waiting at the door for a chance to call Debbie. I had read from Genesis to Numbers and would continue to read the Bible to gain more knowledge. It was time for us to leave the cell and I could call Debbie. I hoped she had some news from Baton Rouge.

I finished talking to Debbie for the morning. She had no news from Baton Rouge. Debbie was hoping to hear something later in the day. I was still in the dark as to exactly why I was in jail and what I needed to do to get out. It still uplifted my soul to hear her voice. I made a covenant with the Lord concerning her. I could hardly wait to fulfill my covenants with the Lord. My strength was back now. I thanked the Lord. Peace would be with me throughout today. Now I would study more. I thanked the Father for giving me my fight back. I was not a victim; I was a child of God. I would fight for what was right. Father, I prayed, let me out of here! I ask Thee in the name of Jesus Christ to show me the way. I will do whatsoever thou ask me to do. I was back in my cell for the next four hours. I tried to sleep a little. My cellmate was asleep. He had not asked me any questions concerning religion, but I saw that he had a copy of the Book of Mormon. He was in the bottom bunk and I had the top bunk. Still, I was unable to sleep. I continued to ask the Lord for a way to get out of jail. I would be out of lock up in about thirty minutes. Then I would be able to talk to Debbie again. I prayed that she had some answers! We were out of the cell and now I could talk to Debbie.

I spoke to Debbie. This thing was wearing on her. By the grace of God, she sent the information to Larry. I extended my hope and prayers to Debbie because I knew this was getting to her. When this thing is over, I would teach her to stand tall when you had to. I told her where all the money we had was located. I was sure we would have to buy our way out of the mess. Debbie had all of our money in place for the war tomorrow; for there was nothing we could do to get out of jail today. I just hoped Debbie could hang in there. Debbie was my only contact with the outside world. Debbie gave me Larry's phone number and I would contact Larry tonight to give him all the information I had so that he would have the best shot in the battle. Larry planned to go to court tomorrow to find out why I was in jail and how I could get out of jail. I prayed that Heavenly Father would be with me in the name of Jesus Christ, Amen.

I called Larry twice and never got him. I emailed Debbie a message to forward to Larry and she did. I got Debbie's email. I tried to inspire Debbie to do more and I thought that she would. I would continue to plead with God to bless Debbie and to make a way for me to get out of here. I would try to go to sleep. It was 9pm, so I read for about an hour. I thanked my Heavenly Father for everything, and prayed Amen.

Day 7

It was a long night. I woke up around 3 am and could not go back to sleep. I prayed to my Father most of the night. It was 5 am and time to eat breakfast and cleanup. Now I was going back to sleep since I did not sleep last night. My cellmate went to court at 8am. I could not hold it in any longer. I cried out to my Heavenly Father in real tears. I have not cried like this since my mother died. I pleaded with my Heavenly Father to make a way for me to get out of jail. I reaffirmed my covenants with Him. I focused all of my spirit to work in His Kingdom. I asked for a blessing for Debbie that she would stay strong. I asked a blessing on the full court system that they could find a way for me to get out of jail. I reaffirmed the vision that the Lord gave me and pleaded with the Lord that the vision was true. I had done all that I could do and the Lord would take it from here. The Lord had given me peace. Thank you, Father. A voice came to my mind while I was sitting there in the door of my cell. I said I am listening for I expected the Lord to speak to me. These words were spoken to my mind. "You wanted to see me. You did not see me. I will do a work for you today so that you will not need to see me and still know that I am." The Lord wanted me to share this vision with Alisa. I have no idea why. There was something about this scripture Deuteronomy 8:18-19 that the Lord wanted me to understand. I was not sure what it was.

> "**18** But thou shalt remember the LORD thy God: for it is he that giveth thee power to get wealth, that he may establish his covenant which he swear unto thy fathers, as it is this day. **19** And it shall be, if thou do at all forget the LORD thy God, and walk after other gods, and serve them, and worship them, I testify against you this day that ye shall surely perish." (KJV)

Then the voice said to me, "Write what you have just heard for it is correct." I was thinking, "Is it possible that the Lord would deliver me from this jail today or tomorrow?" Surely, I could never question Jesus Christ again nor even questioned him in that manner. For the Lord would have done exactly what he had said in the vision. I had always asked to see Jesus and at this moment I should not ask any more. Then, there must be a work He wants me to do. He used my logic to confirm himself in me. He knows how I think and how I operate. The Lord used these things to clear any doubts from my heart as to who He is. Then another vision came to my mind. These words were spoken, "I will remove you from this jail, just as I revealed it to you. Then you will never doubt Me, and you will know who I am without seeing me. You will see Me, when I decide. But now you will know Me without seeing, which is greater than seeing." The Lord was right and I knew that this was the purpose of this whole ordeal. Now, I had to wait for the time when the Lord would deliver me from this jail.

My cellmate returned from court. He was getting out today. This was great. I was glad he was getting out but now I would get a new cellmate. I wasn't sure who it would be. This didn't make me happy. There had been a number of fights among cellmates. We had been in our cell all day. Since this was a court day, there were not enough guards to watch us when we were outside of our cells. I had not been able to make a phone call yet. I waited now to hear from the Lord. I was going to get out of jail on Thursday according to an earlier vision. Therefore, I waited with a prayer in my heart. Finally, I was getting out of this cell. I called Debbie. She cried for the first time that I knew of. I told her to be strong, that we would get out of this. I knew this was very tough for her. I had to get off the phone to make other calls to try to get out of jail. I called Larry four times with no answer. I was very concerned that no one was working on my case. I decided that if I did not reach Larry tonight, I would get Debbie to contact Roy Maughun another lawyer I knew. I began to think about the vision that I would get out of jail on Thursday. I thought, "What if I do not get out on Thursday, then what about the vision?"

I was back in my cell for the night. I was lying on my bed and I got mad. I remembered that the Lord had given me great talents and right now, I was not using those talents. A vision came to me and I heard these words, "Do something for yourself with whatever you have." I was sure this message came from the Lord via the Holy Ghost. So now, I went on the offensive. The Lord would back me! My cellmate had just left and I had his number. On his way out, he told me he would study the Bible and the Book of Mormon and find out for himself what was true. I told him, "This is the only way to know."

Now if there was a work that the Lord wanted me to do, I no longer had to ask to see Him first, but only had to do what He said. This was my lesson for today and I heard it. This was so frustrating for me. I had no control of anything right now! I did not want to write any more that day.

Chapter 10

About this time, I joined the United States Air Force. I took all of my materials, all of my religious research, and all of my journals with me to basic training in San Antonio, Texas. I thought I would have personal time to continue my studies. I went through basic training and after it was over all of my belongings were returned to me, with one exception. The United States Air Force had destroyed all of my journals, the Quran, and three years of work. All of it was gone. They had thrown it all away! I was sure that the Air Force felt I did not have time to be dealing with religious stuff in their military. I lost all of it. I was completely devastated.

Even though it was a great loss to me to lose all of my papers, books and other items, I was still happy. I was in the military, I had a job, which made it possible for me to marry my high school sweetheart, and I had a daughter named Tiffany. Tiffany was the most important person in my whole world. More important than anything was this bright-eyed, sweet little girl and she was my baby. I loved her more than life itself. I could never imagine ever loving anyone as much as I loved my daughter.

Life went on and several years later, I had a son, who we named Kenneth Jr. I had my two kids, I had my wife, and I had everything I had ever wanted out of life. I never thought about religion at this time.

As far as I was concerned, religion was for someone else, not me and not my family.

If you do not know, when you are in the military things can change drastically, very quickly without warning. This is exactly what happened to me. Before I could enjoy my family, I received orders to spend a year in Korea. Because the assignment was for twelve months, I was not able to take my family. What a nightmare. While I was in Korea, an interesting thing happened. I met a Korean girl named Chun. She could speak some English. I do not know why, but our conversations quickly turned to religion. Through her, I learned about the different religions that existed in Korea. I asked Chun to take me to meet some of the local religious leaders in the town of Taegu. She took me to this place to meet some monks. We were waiting on the swings in a playground area. We sat there waiting for them to come by. We waited for about thirty minutes and then I saw them. There were about four or five of them dressed like monks, of course. Their hair was cut very short. They wore brown robes. They walked as if they were in a great hurry. They walked in a straight line and did not make a sound. I wanted to talk to them and ask questions about what they believed. I began to approach them. Chun blocked my path. She informed me that I could not talk to them. I asked her to ask the monks questions for me. She seemed to be somewhat afraid to approach them. Yet, I was able to get her to ask them a couple of questions. She asked the questions, but they did not respond. They kept walking as if they had to get somewhere quickly. She told me that they never talk. I asked Chun if she had ever heard of Jesus Christ. She said some Americans had mentioned the name, but she did not know anything about him or Christianity. I never discussed it with her again.

While I was in Korea serving my country, my personal world came apart at the seams. It almost seemed that in an instant my family was gone. My new assignment was in Shreveport, Louisiana. My wife moved back to Mississippi with my children. In my life, nothing was more important than my children. You could take everything else away from me except my children. Their mom knew how I felt about my children. She knew that I could become quite emotional and irrational when it came to my children. She also knew that in my military career, I had done things that were very dangerous, complex and confidential. Many people had their lives changed because of secret things they had done in their military careers. She began to feel fearful and paranoid that I could cause something to happen to her. Although I never discussed it with her, I think this was the reason she felt the need to put some distance between us. She took my kids and moved to Mississippi. This was extremely painful for me. Although I cared deeply for my wife, I also felt that people have to do what makes them happy. If a divorce was what she wanted then I would let her go. I would not stand in her way. My children were a different story. She knew that somehow I would devise a way to get them away from her so they could grow up with me. After all, she was the one that wanted the divorce. I felt she was determined to get to Mississippi because she believed I would not do anything in the town where my parents lived. I think that was an ingenious calculation on her part.

Ironically, I had a lawyer in Louisiana who was unique. He and I spent a great deal of time discussing my options on how to get my children back. Unfit mother was out of the picture. My children's mom was a very good mom who took very good care of the children. They wanted for nothing. Therefore, I was out of legal options.

I was talking to my lawyer one day and I asked him, "Look, Stan, I know you know how I can get my children back." Now, I was never upset about my wife leaving, but I was upset that she took my children. Therefore, what I really wanted was for her to give me my kids and she could go do whatever she wanted to do as far as I was concerned. She could just go do it without my kids. I lived by several philosophies, one of them was "If you are not happy with something in your life then you should change it." Therefore, I did not have any problem with her changing her life because she felt that she was not happy.

I told my lawyer, "I must have my children and you must give me any legal option that I have. Otherwise, I was going to take my children illegally." My lawyer said very quietly, "Here's what I want you to do. I want you to go into Mississippi. Do not let anyone know that you are coming to town. I want you to pick the children up from school. Act normally with them. Give them no cause to be suspicious. Then drive as cautiously and as safely as you can back to Louisiana. In essence I want you to steal your children." Until that moment, I thought it was impossible for something to render me speechless. Then he said this and I was speechless. My mind went into orbit. It took off imagining all sorts of scenarios. First, I could not believe my lawyer was suggesting this to me. He was a professional, a man of the law. Second, how could I pull this off? Could I pull this off? Could I be bold enough to steal my own children?

"You want me to steal them?" I asked.

My lawyer stated, "Well, you wanted a way to get your children. I am giving you a way to get your children. So don't get upset!"

He continued, "You should also be aware that if you are caught, I will not acknowledge giving you any advice about any of this. You will totally be on your own."

I thought stealing my children would be very painful for a lot of people: including my wife, my mother-in-law, and my mother. Yet, even knowing this I found myself planning out the details of how to do this. This was going to take an enormous amount of planning. Everything would have to be planned to the minute. I could not believe what I was doing. I was actually sitting here contemplating stealing my children from their mother. I replayed in my mind what he had just said, "This is what you can do, go to Mississippi and steal the children. Now if you should be able to get them it is imperative that you get out of Mississippi into Louisiana as safely and as quickly as you can. Then you could sue your wife for abandonment and win your children legally through the courts. Now if you get caught in Mississippi by the authorities, you will go to jail."

I thought, wow, that is very interesting. I was really considering it. What I needed was a car, money and time. Then I needed a way to get back to Louisiana without the highway patrol picking me up. This was not going to be a simple task, but for my children I would do anything except bring physical harm to their mother or them.

After about a week, my plan was in place. I went to work on Tuesday night. This could not be done on the weekend. I got off at about 2:30am and borrowed a car from a friend who would ask no questions. I left for Mississippi around 3:30 am. I needed to arrive there at the time my kids would be in school, their mom would be at work and few people who knew me would be out and about. I went to the day care center and picked up Kenneth, my son. Next, I went to the school and I picked up Tiffany, my daughter. Then I went to the store where their mother worked. I went and met with her; I did not want her to get off work and not be able to find her children. The conversation went something like this, "Look, I have the children and I'm taking them back to Louisiana with me. You want a different life and that is fine with me, but that does not mean my children and I have to suffer and be separated because of what you want. So I'm taking the children and will see you later." The horror of what I just said showed on her face. She responded, "You cannot take my children!" I did not wait to listen to anything after that. I got in the car and took off. Now the key was that I had to make it back over the Mississippi line before the highway patrolmen caught me. I knew that I would be put in jail for stealing or kidnapping my own children if I was caught. I went a different way back to Louisiana, because I knew that Kathy would have the highway patrol looking for the children and me. She expected me to travel through the Southern part of Mississippi to get to Louisiana. I took the northern route to Louisiana, which was about two hundred miles farther to get into Louisiana. However, I had to go this way. I had the added advantage of them not knowing what kind of car we were driving. My kids were so excited because they were with their father now. We were talking, singing and having a lot of fun. We were just being completely silly and having loads of fun. Tiffany was the most happy of all because she was a Daddy's girl. I really, really loved her. I had missed them so much. I had missed being with them so much. I had not realized it until right now. The trip was a hoot.

We were blessed that we made it to Louisiana safely and I took them to my townhouse. I told Tiffany, "Tiffany, this is your house now and you have control. You have got to help me raise and care for your brother." She did not back down at all. She was a big girl and I knew she would do well. We had some great times. I would get up each morning and get Tiffany off to school. Then I would head to work and drop Kenneth off at day care. My neighbor noticed that I had the children with me now. She asked if she could do anything to help me. Some days she would cook for us when she knew I was having a particularly tough time. I do not know how she knew, but she knew and I was truly grateful. Tiffany would set the table and we would eat. We would talk about the day's activities and challenges. It was great. After a few weeks, things became more difficult. After all, I was taking care of two kids and working at the same time. I talked with my neighbor, and my neighbor said, "Okay, when your daughter gets out of school she can stay with me and I'll keep your son during the day." Therefore, my neighbor kept Kenneth during the day and when Tiffany got out of school, she would walk home with the other kids and go to the neighbor's house. I would come home about six o'clock and being in the military my schedule would change often. These two kids were so happy and I was so happy, but every day Kathy would call me and ask me to "bring my children home." For some reason, she was afraid to come to Louisiana to get the kids. She always felt I did evil things in the military. I had a top-secret clearance, so she was nervous about the things I did. She would say things like, "I might come up missing and no one would ever find me." She forgot that I would never do anything to the mother of my children.

Tiffany was the mother of the house now. She tried to cook dinner but she knew very little. She tried and that was all that mattered. Tiffany was ten years old and Kenneth was four. Man, it was just great! It was an unbelievable life. I was so happy to have my children. Then the worst thing that could possibly happen happened. My mom began to call me trying to get me to bring the children back. I believe Kathy called my mom and got her to call me. Kathy knew that my mom was the only person who could get me to do anything. Every day, my mom would call me and say, "You need to bring those children back to their mother because children need to be with their mother. You need to bring them back. You can't keep doing this." This was the one time I was not going to listen to anyone. There was no way I would give up my children. I had already spoken to the lawyer and he was ready to file the necessary paperwork so that I could keep my children. I was trying to raise two kids with an ever-changing work schedule and every day my mom would call and work on me to get me to bring the children back to their mother. Finally, my mom wore me down enough to get me to bring them back to their mom in Mississippi. I think I kept them for about two months. I remember it was one of the saddest days of my life when I told Tiffany that I was going to have to take them back. Tiffany said to me, "But daddy we don't want to go back. We want to stay with you." I said, "I know, I know and I want you to stay, but your mother needs you. She needs both of you at home because it's very difficult for her to not be with you guys." Even at that time, I cared about other people's feelings more than my own. Even though I wanted to keep my children, I also knew I had to take them back because it was destroying their mother. Kathy was never a bad mother. She was not a very good wife, but she was a very good mother. My mom had worked on me enough that I finally decided to pack them up and take them home. I took them back to their mom's house. Tiffany was devastated. She really enjoyed being the woman of the house. It was so painful for me to do this, but at the time, it seemed like it was the best thing to do.

I hugged and kissed them goodbye, dropped them off and drove back to Louisiana. I was still in the Air Force. I had to get back to work. I went to my new life, a life without my children. I was trying to do something to keep my mind busy so I would not have to think. I started going fishing daily. This continued for about six weeks. Every day I would go fishing. I caught so many fish that after my freezer was full I would give them away to my friends. I did not care what happened at work, I could hardly wait to get off so I could go fishing. Unbelievably, as soon as I took the children back I got a permanent schedule that was stable. Go figure!

Then, all of a sudden I showed up at work one day and found out that I was about to be sent to Japan for two years. A couple of days passed, and then I discovered it had been extended to three years. My first thought was that I couldn't leave my children for that long! What was I going to do? They would grow up without me in their lives. What was I going to do?

Therefore, I made a trip to Mississippi and tried my best to talk to Kathy to get her to try to work out our situation. There were other people involved by this time, but I just could not leave my children. I just could not. Therefore, I tried to convince Kathy that working out our marriage was the right thing to do. I needed to convince her that going to Japan with me would give us the fresh start we needed to keep our family together. I worked with my lawyer to begin the process of getting everyone's passport prepared for the trip. We were able to pull everything together. All the paperwork was in order. My orders were processed to include my wife and my children. I was going to get to see my children grow up. My family was set to go to Japan. Everything was set. I had to commit to the third year in Japan to take them with me. I went to see them and talk with Kathy about a week before it was time to leave. I went to move them back to Louisiana with me because our departure for Japan was out of Louisiana. I was still working on trying to let her know how great it would be for us to do this. I told her that we could leave all the mistakes we both made here in Mississippi and start over with a clean slate. She said to me, "The children and I are not going to Japan with you. I just cannot do it." I replied, "Please let me tell you, and I want you to understand this, I care about you and I love my children, but I feel that if you don't go to Japan with me then that will be the end for us. I feel that it is certain we will be headed for divorce if you do not go with me."

I drove back to Louisiana, having only a week before I had to leave for Japan. I met with my Commander and asked, "Is there any way possible that I can take my children?" Of course, the military was totally against the idea. I thought, there must be a way to take my children, but there was no time. Yet, there was one thing I was able to pull off before leaving for Japan. I met with my lawyer and I got the divorce done. I was now divorced, I was leaving the country and I was going to be gone at least two years and maybe three. I was leaving my children behind. I felt angry and empty. This was the most painful thing I had ever gone through.

Now this was a very difficult time for me. I knew now that I would never know the joy of my children growing up in the house with me. I would never help them with their homework. I would never be able to go to parent-teacher meetings. I would not get to walk them to school. I would not be able to take them to ball practice. I would never be the father that I wanted to be to them. They would grow up without me. I would never be able to teach them the things that I had learned. All those potentially good memories were gone now. They would grow up without my direct influence. Who would they be-come? I remember sitting in St Louis, Missouri on an airplane. There were about 500 people on this plane because many people were taking their families with them to Japan. I was sitting there on the plane and reality hit me. This was it. I would never have my children again. Tiffany was my first child, my daughter. Tiffany was my whole world. Now I loved my son more than anything in the world, but Tif-fany came first. I was seventeen when she was born and I just was not sure how I could go on without her. I was sitting there on the plane and I began to cry. It was so painful. I thought that if there was a God somewhere, this God was punishing me for all of the things that I had done wrong and now he was taking my children from me. If there was not a God then this was just the way it worked sometimes. I hardened my heart that day. Otherwise, I could not survive the pain that I was going through. The plane took off and that was the end of that for me. I knew that my life would never be the same again.

Chapter 11

Day 8 & Day 9

The day started as usual, I was locked up! Then I had to stand at my cell door to be counted. I watched the inmates come out of their cells to take medicine. Then the inmates went back into their cells. Then, I waited for one hour and we ate breakfast and cleaned our cells. However, today would be different. I had two lawyers trying to find out why I am here. I was sure one of them would find out something, then I would take care of whatever the situation was and get out of here tomorrow. I was waiting for our break, so that I could call Debbie. I finally got to the phone. I called my lawyer first. He answered the phone. I couldn't believe what my lawyer was telling me via the phone. He said there were two issues in court against me. One was that I owed a bank $2800.00. The bank filed a case of fraud against me. In the second case, someone stated that my company had $8,555.00 in outstanding checks. This company was closed over a year ago. The lawyer told me that he was not sure who the people were but there was no chance that I could get out of jail. He told me that I missed a court date about twelve months ago. When I missed the court date, there was a warrant issued for my arrest by the court. The court system would not allow me to get out of jail unless I came to Baton Rouge. The issue was not the money I owed, but me missing the court date. I told him to get me bail and I would fly to Baton Rouge and come to court. The lawyer told me that I would have to stay in jail until the state of Louisiana came to pick me up. I asked him, "How long does this take?" He told me it could be up to six weeks! I thought, "You have got to be kidding!" He was not. I hung up the phone as tears rolled down my cheeks. My heart could not handle this. Through all my tears and with great pain in my heart, I began to ask the Lord for help. Then I went to work! I had to get my hands on $11,355. I did not want to talk to anyone. I only wanted to go to my cell and be alone. At this time, I did not have a roommate. I did not read anything. I did not come back out of my cell the rest of the day. I slept all I could from that point on until the next day. I knew I had to go to war. I needed rest to prepare myself for the long haul.

Day 9

I was up early and ready to go to war. The Lord had given me strength. They counted me at the door without having to wake me. Breakfast was done. Clean up was done. I wanted to get to the phone to try to find the money to pay off the debt. The lovers (inmates who have been here many times) went to the phones first. They called their wives and girlfriends who were accustomed to this type of relationship. I was waiting to get to the phone! It was time for me to use the talents that the Lord had given me. These guys were taking too long on the phone. They were talking to their wives and girlfriends. I decided to go get a shower. I was now in the shower. My mind was running at a thousand miles a minute. I was now out of the shower and had gotten dressed. Now I had to get to the phone. One of the lovers got off the phone. I was trying to dial Debbie. Then the guard called my name and told me I had a visitor on the visitor monitor. In this jail when a person wanted to visit, they had to visit via a video device. This device was very similar to a Skype session. Now I had a visitor. It was my Bishop. I was so glad to speak with him. It brought comfort just speaking with my Bishop. He said things to me that no man has said to me before. He offered me hope and peace. I asked him to take care of Debbie. He told me the whole church would be there for Debbie and me. This brought great comfort to me. When we ended our visit, I knew the Lord, through His Church, would take care of Debbie. My Bishop even offered to contact my employer to attempt to save my job. However, saving my job did not matter to me. What matter is that he told me, "The church would take care of Debbie." What a system the Lord has in place through His Church.

Now it was time to focus on getting this money. I got on the phone with a friend of mine. I told him I needed $5000.00. Without any hesitation, he said you got it. I asked him to give it to Debbie. He said he would give Debbie the money today. I said thank you and I would get it back to him. He said I know you will. I have not known this guy long, yet I knew he would come through for me. I also had some money stashed back. I was very close to having the money I needed, but I didn't know if it would matter. The court system in Baton Rouge didn't care about the money. They wanted me to come to Baton Rouge because they felt that I had disrespected the court system by not showing up on my court date. I was prepared to do my best to get the people paid that I owed money to. The bad thing was that I didn't know who to pay! Debbie and my lawyers were trying to find out who needed to be paid. I thanked Jesus for strengthening me. It was 5:30 pm now and I had been reading in Mark in the Bible. I started a fast. I was fasting for the following:

1. Tomorrow, Debbie and the lawyers could find out who I owed money to so we could pay them.
2. That my check would be deposited into our bank account tonight. This was my normal pay date.
3. That my lawyer would find a way to get me out of jail without me going to Louisiana.

Even though it might not matter if I payoff this debt, as far as me getting out of jail, it was something I wanted to do because it was the right thing to do.

I was back in my cell for about three hours. We were back out of the cells for another break. I was watching a football game and waiting for a phone to open so I could call Debbie. I was running every name through my mind to try to come up with people I might owe money. The Lord allowed me to think of someone. In my construction business, my guys would go to this store to cash their checks. Before I left Baton Rouge, thirteen months ago, I deposited some checks into my business account and paid my workers. About three months later, I confirmed all checks had cleared and closed the account. Could this have been the bank? Could something have gone wrong? A phone opened. I called Debbie and told her to call every bank we ever banked with to see if we owed them money. I asked Debbie to call the store where the workers went to cash their checks. Maybe something went wrong there. I could not remember the name of the store. Debbie took care of the mortgage and I gave her information on checking where all of our other money was located. Debbie also picked up the $5000. All I wanted was to pay the people I owed so I could get out of jail. The Lord always issues justice and mercy. The justice was that I was in jail. I had done something that got me here. Mercy was what I sought. I got off the phone with Debbie and she had her work cut out for her. I loved Debbie so much and looked to the day when we could be back together. I was back in my cell and looking forward to getting some sleep. I had taken all the steps I could for today. I said good night.

Chapter 12

About sixteen hours later, we landed in Japan. The military assigns a person to welcome you to the new base. My escort met me at the airport and asked me, "Where is your family?" I told them that my family did not come. Everyone was cool with that statement. I did not say anymore.

In Japan, I went on with my new life. I worked like crazy because I had nothing else to do. I had no religion, I had no God, I had no wife, and I had no children. As far as I was concerned, I had absolutely nothing. I did not want a girlfriend, I did not want to date anyone, and I did not want to do anything but work. I worked around the clock. I worked on weekends. I worked when I did not have to. It did not matter to me. I worked all the time because that was the only thing that could ease my pain.

I never talked to my mom or anyone else to let them know how much pain I was in. This was the time that I developed the technique of turning inward. When things went wrong around me, I turned inward and communicated with no one and this protected me from all pain.

As I was spending my time in Japan, a beautiful country, many things were going on and I met this young girl. She worked with me.

Her name was Terri. She was eighteen. She and I became very good friends because I wanted to protect her from all of the guys that were in Japan. I needed her also to run interference for me because I did not want anyone to know anything about me. I just disliked people knowing anything about me. I would have her come by my house to pick up my car so that no one would come to my house. People began to think that I was dating her. She was such a special girl to me. She never knew that I used her to run interference for me. Terri protected me for months from other women. She was very pretty and everyone thought, "There is no need to talk with him. He has that pretty young girl!"

I had been in Japan for about a year now and I ran into this special lady named Debbie. I had originally met her when I first got to Japan. I remember shaking her hand and she said "I'm Sergeant Carswell," and I said, "I'm Sergeant Holloway." That was pretty much it. I recall a friend of mine really liked her and I was trying to help him with dating her. I had no interest in her or anyone else. I did not want to be interested in anyone. I did not want anything. I was just trying to find my way through life after losing my children.

Debbie used to come by my desk a lot. Debbie worked for the squadron commander. She and I worked together on special tasks. Our role was to relocate and setup mobile computer systems should the base be attacked and destroyed. We began to work together a lot. However, I still had no interest in Debbie because she was such a nice woman and being around me was not a good idea. She needed to find a nice husband and I was not nice at all. We began to talk and she would bring me food at work because she knew I worked so much. She would bring me food and leave it at my desk. I did not think much about it. I did not even say thank you or anything. I had no idea why she brought me food, but she did. I had no idea that this was her way of saying she was attracted to me. At this time, a relationship was not on my mind at all. Debbie would always come by my desk to see me. I just thought she was a nice woman.

One day I was at my house and I was barbequing with a friend of mine named Lee. It snowed about six months out of the year so I learned to adjust anything I would normally do as if it were not snowing. I had tried to set Lee up with Debbie. However, it did not work out. I was one of the few people that Debbie would talk with. Debbie was a very unique woman. She did and said exactly what she wanted. Guys labeled her as crazy because she was so straightforward about what she wanted. So the guys were a little intimidated by her.

My phone rang while I was barbequing. Lee answered the phone and with a strange look, he said, "This is Debbie."

I said, "Debbie who?"

He then said, "It's Sergeant Carswell."

I wondered why she would be calling me. Debbie knew that I liked this professional football player named Eric Dickerson, I answered the phone and she talked to me about football and a few other things. Then I hung the phone up and Lee looked at me with this funny look on his face and said, "What's up?"

I answered, "I don't know what that was about. I don't know why she is calling me."

Lee looked at me with a look of disbelief on his face and said, "You really don't get it do you?"

I said, "Get what?"

He said, "Man she likes you."

I was completely floored. That had never occurred to me. Immediately I thought that it was not a good idea for her. No one should like me, not now. I was not the person that someone should like right now. I did know Debbie. She was such a nice lady. I just did not want to mess up her life. As I saw it, my life was already messed up. I did not want to dump all my baggage on her.

Debbie continued to talk with me at work. We started talking on the phone after work. Some nights we would talk all night. We would get off the phone when it was time to go to work. During one conversation we talked about food and she happened to mention that she was a great cook. Therefore, I asked her "When will you invite me to dinner?" A couple of weeks later she invited me to her house for dinner. I went to her house and I thought I was there for a different reason. She had actually cooked and we actually ate and talked about a lot of different things. I found her to be more interesting that I originally thought. After talking for a while, she said goodnight and I went home. I thought about Debbie most of the night. I kept thinking that I didn't have time for this. I didn't have time for any kind of relationship. She intrigued me because she was such a sweet person and I began to have an interest in her. I began to talk to her more and more. It was not long after that dinner we began to date. I would take her many places all across the country of Japan. She didn't know why I took her to little Buddhist churches. She didn't know that I was there to try and find out what the Buddhist people believe. Again, I had an opportunity to talk to people who were Buddhist. Now these were not monks, but practicing Buddhists. I was studying them, but I did not want Debbie to know. I was not sure what she would think. I figured because she was from Alabama and probably a strong Christian, I was not sure what she would think if she knew about my lack of religious beliefs. Debbie never really knew why we traveled so much.

Everything was great. Then all of a sudden one day we decided that maybe we should get married. We had been dating for about six months or so. I thought, "Oh no, no, no I don't want to be married to anybody. I know she is a nice lady and she will make someone a good wife, but not me." Therefore, I did some things to break us up.

In the past, I had a relationship with a girl named Georgia who was a little younger than I was. She still had feelings for me. I tried to make it clear to her that I was not interested in anything long-term. I got Georgia to pretend that she was pregnant by me. We created this plan to "leak" this information to Debbie. Well it was not pretty. Debbie handled things very well with Georgia. Debbie and I decided that we needed some time away from each other after this incident. About a week later, I called Debbie and apologized. I did not want her to dislike me, but I intentionally broke us up because I did not want her to get caught up in my situation. Nevertheless, she was just such a sweet person that we dated for several months and decided to get married.

Since we were out of the United States and on a military installation, we had to get the permission of the base commander. Now here was the incredible thing. We made the appointment to speak with the Commander to inform him of our plans. He gave a verbal approval. We began addressing the necessary paperwork. Then I was hit with some very interesting news. The base admin clerk stated, "Oh no, Sergeant Holloway, you cannot get married."

I asked, "Well, why not?"

The clerk said, "Because you are already married."

I said, "No… no I'm not. I am divorced! Let me get my divorce papers."

I went back to my house to get my divorce papers. I presented the divorce papers to the clerk. The divorce papers had the official court seal and everything on it. The clerk said, "Look, we have checked with the state of Louisiana and you are married."

I said, "But I cannot be married! Here are my divorce papers."

Debbie was devastated because she thought that I had purposely lied about being divorced.

As soon as I got home, I got on the phone and started calling the United States to try to figure out what the heck had happened. Finally, I was able to speak to the lawyer's office that I worked with initially for the divorce in Louisiana. They informed me that although my paperwork was done and I had a copy, in order for the divorce to be official, the lawyer had to file the papers with the court. The lawyer was killed in a traffic accident on his way to court to file the divorce papers. So the divorce papers were never filed. All of the lawyer's cases went to some state board to complete them. This board had been trying to contact me for over a year to let me know what happened. They were contacting me at my old address. They did not realize that I was out of the country. I finally spoke to someone over the phone. After we talked for about five minutes, I stated, "So you're telling me that I'm still married?"

The person on the phone said, "Yes sir, you are still married, because the paperwork was never filed with the court system."

This was unbelievable! I replied, "I cannot believe this. How can this be possible? What am I supposed to do? I am out of the country."

She said, "I am sorry, sir. The only thing I can tell you is that you will need to get another lawyer and start the process over." I was heartbroken. On top of that, Debbie refused to talk to me because she thought I had lied to her about my marital status. She did not believe that I did not know. She was upset. I could not blame her. I was upset also.

I left Japan because my enlistment was up. I left Debbie in Japan and I told her, "I'm going back to America and I'm going to get this whole thing straightened out. And if you still want to marry me, come home in six months and we will get married." I went back to America.

Kathy had always known that we were not divorced. We had spoken many times about the kids and she never shared this information. She continued to parade around town as my wife. I was really upset with her because I felt her angle was money and the privileges she had by being a military wife. If something happened to me while I was serving, as my wife she was the beneficiary of a great sum of money.

When I got back to America all of a sudden, Kathy wanted to work things out. She wanted to save our marriage. Of course my answer was, "No, that's not going to happen."

I reminded her of my original offer right before I was leaving for Japan. "I told you if you did not go to Japan, our relationship was over."

So she tried to use the kids as leverage or an excuse, I am not sure what she was thinking. She knew my children meant everything to me. What she did not realize is that I had accepted things the way they were. I knew that my relationship with my children was gone forever. I did not like that fact but it took me a long time to accept. She knew that I did not see her as I once did. I told her I would always love her but there could never be the relationship that we once had. I filed for and got a second divorce. I got divorced from the same woman twice without a second marriage. Needless to say, everything was done and I left Mississippi and moved to Memphis, Tennessee. While I was in Memphis, Debbie came there after about six months. She came in and we looked at each other and did not know what to say. Yet, we headed for the courthouse to get married. I asked her, "Now, are you sure you want to marry me?"

She answered, "Well, I'm not sure I want to marry anybody right now because I'm not sure I want to get married at all." Debbie had been through a divorce also. She still had those unhappy memories from the first marriage. We talked for several hours trying to make the best decision. We ended up heading for the courthouse in downtown Memphis to be married. We almost talked ourselves out of getting married. We got married and we moved from Memphis to Atlanta the same day. Debbie's thirty days of leave was over. She went back to Japan for six more months while I tried to establish us in Atlanta. No one I worked with in Atlanta believed that I was married because they never saw Debbie at any of our company functions. They thought I made her up.

Debbie came to the United States from Japan after six months. She was stationed in Blytheville, Arkansas. She still owed the military 12 months to complete her enlistment. We went back and forth visiting each other. Debbie and I were married for eighteen months before we lived together. I do not know what kind of situation that was, but that is the way we did it. It worked out fine. Then we finally lived together, we built a house, and then had a baby. We had AJ. I was so happy when AJ was born. Just four years earlier, I was sitting in St Louis on a flight to Japan. I knew I had lost my children forever. I asked God, if there was such a being, if He could give me another son. I knew I had done a lot of bad things in my life, but maybe after my punishment was over, maybe I could have another son. Amazingly, I did have a belief that there was a God or super power. I just did not believe in Christianity and the Bible.

So now, I was in living in Douglasville, Georgia. I had my wife, I had my son, I had my career and everything was good. Debbie came to me one day and said, "I want to try and do something special every Monday."

I said, "Well, what do you want to do?"

She said, "I want to do something called Family Home Evening."

I asked her, "What in the world is Family Home Evening?"

Debbie said, "Well, it's this idea where we spend time together on Mondays, I saw it on TV. It was a video and I ordered it so we can try it". I was thinking ok fine whatever. Because whatever she asked me, I would do it. It did not make any difference to me. My only interest was in making money. That was it. Whatever Debbie wanted, she could have it. It did not make me any difference. My focus was on money. Money became the key to my life. You see everyone has something that is the key to their life and most people, I knew, centered on the concept of Jesus Christ and Heaven. Well my whole life was centered on money. Money was constant as far as I was concerned. Every decision I made was based on money because it was the only consistent thing that I knew. Whatever Debbie wanted, I would make happen. In return, Debbie would never interfere with my pursuit of money. We were a prefect team.

Debbie got her video concerning the concept of Family Home Evening. She never asked me for help in setting up this family home evening program. We did it. One day, I came home and there were these notes on my door. They were little yellow sticky notes and I just took them and threw them in the garbage. Sometimes they were yellow, sometimes orange and sometimes pink. Whatever color they were they all went into the garbage. I did not know why Debbie never saw or was aware that there were notes being left on the door. The second time I came home and those notes were there I just threw them in the garbage again.

I was a software consultant. I designed computer software. I was very good at what I did and I was at the top of my career. I was making six figures and everything was going great for our family. I worked in Brazil and I had an interesting life. I had a lot of things going on. I later took a consulting contract to work in Indianapolis, IN. I took the job in Indianapolis because that is where the money sent us. We lived in Indianapolis for two years and my contract there was completed. Now it was time to go home to Atlanta. We had lived in Atlanta and had rented our house out while we were away. Just before leaving Indianapolis, Debbie said to me, "I do not want to go back to Atlanta. I want to move to Louisiana." I thought what the heck; I do not want to go to Louisiana. I did not want to go back to the South. I just did not want to go there, but for Debbie I would do anything. Therefore, if that was what she wanted then that was what she got. So we moved to Louisiana to be close to her sister Sarah and our families.

Upon planning our move to Louisiana, the reason I did not want to go to the South happened. I was buying a house that had about thirty-seven acres of land with uncut timber. I was going to buy the house, sell the timber, and then move right back out of Louisiana. It was a $300,000 deal for me. That was my plan. When I got to Louisiana... I am going to say point blank the way things were in the South. When I got to Louisiana the white people there were not going to let a black man buy that much land because they did not want me to have it. That would be too much progress for a black man to obtain in that area. Therefore, they did everything possible to stop me from buying the house. In fact, they did stop me from getting it even though I had the money. That is why I did not want to go back to the South. I did not want to deal with this type of situation, but we decided to stay. People would come to me and ask me, "Why would you move from Atlanta or Indianapolis to this little town of four hundred people?" I said to them as a joke, "God was playing a trick on me." I cannot believe I used words like that but that was what I said. There was no reason for me to be in Louisiana. I had to give up too much to go to this place!

Chapter 13

Day 10

got very little sleep last night, the same as yesterday. Wake up was at 5:00 am. I got out of bed and stood at the door of the cell to be counted due to a guard shift change. I lay back into the bed for about an hour and then went to breakfast. I ate breakfast and cleaned the cell, then waited another two hours to be let out of the cell. I asked the Lord to just let me sleep a little while, but I couldn't sleep. I prayed throughout the night that Debbie would be able to find out who I owed money. The money was in place to make the payments but we didn't know who to pay yet. I felt that in order to have any chance to get out of jail I needed to pay off this debt, even though my lawyer told me it would not matter. I could hardly wait to hear what Debbie had found out. Finally, I was out of my cell. I could call Debbie now. Debbie was doing well. She told me she had lost eight pounds. I was not sure if it was from working out or from just worrying so much. Debbie had lined up all the banks to call and I told her to call the Alby's store. This was the store where my workers cashed their checks. I was so excited because we were making some steps in the right direction. Yeah! Debbie was headed to work now and she would make the phone calls later today. I would call her later today when I got out for the next session. I went outside for the first time today. Across from each jail bay was a 40 x 40 cage. Cage was the best word I had for this workout area. The space was within the building compound. On two sides were cement walls about 35 feet high. On the other two sides were glass walls. So today, I decided to get a little sun and work out a little. In the cage, we walked around and tried to get some physical exercise. Fifteen minutes of exercise and then we were headed back to our cells. I was holding up the best I could. In fact, all of us here were doing the best we could. I focused my mind to my time in Korea. There, I lived in a Korean compound for one year. I had some tough times there. So being in jail did not even compare to Korea. These past experiences strengthened me. I went back to my cell and waited for lunch. Usually we got some free time, about an hour, after eating lunch when I could call Debbie to check on the status of things. It was lunchtime. I picked up my food and went back to my cell to eat. The food was not bad this time. I ate a good amount of the food after completing a fast. I had been feeling down for the last half hour. I was down because this was another weekend that I would not see Debbie. I was going to do better. I had to keep moving forward for my family and myself. I needed to start preparing for what I would do once I was out of here. There was a lot of work to do in order to catch up again financially.

We were let out of our cells and I got Debbie on the phone. Now things were turning strange. Debbie had called all the banks that we have ever had an account. One bank said I owed them $48.00. Well I knew this was not the right bank. Debbie talked to the actual bank the lawyer said filed the $2800 claim. Debbie said the people at the bank said we did not owe them any money. They said they never filed a case against me. It is hard to believe that my lawyer said, "This is the bank that was on the summons." Debbie had plans to call other banks to try to find out something. Debbie also called the Alby's store. The store manager checked and said we did not owe them anything, but I knew I owed somebody something! Otherwise, why would I be in jail? This was not looking good. Debbie and I both would continue to fast and pray. I asked Debbie to call the city and sheriff departments of Baton

Rouge to see if they could tell her anything. Now, my name was being called by the guard. I had to get off the phone. The guard was sending me to be fingerprinted and saliva tested. I thought it was Louisiana coming to get me. "Father, why has Thou forsaken me?" I gave my all to serve You for the past twelve years! Yet I knew my Father would never forsake me. I needed to stay focused and make it through this. The state of Louisiana had thirty days to pick me up. This meant that if they didn't show up by October 8th, I would have to be released from jail. I would fight to the end. I said, "My Heavenly Father, strengthen me for this fight! My Heavenly Father, hear my prayers and deliver me to a merciful end. Oh, how great Thou art! How great Thou art!"

I was back in my cell now. I would be able to talk to Debbie again that night. I spoke with an older guy, who was locked up, to ask him to be my cellmate. I knew that someone would be placed in my cell and I wanted to try to have some input. I knew it was Friday. Each Friday many people would be arrested and brought to jail. I did not want just anyone as a cellmate. The guy said yes and he moved into my cell. He looked like an Indian. Well, it was break time and I was going to call Debbie to get an update. I hoped she had some news. Debbie said the first bank she called earlier today called her back. The bank found that they had bought out the bank that was on the summons. This was why we could not find them. The woman was just visiting the closed building when Debbie called earlier. She took it upon herself to look into the records of the bank that they had purchased and found this information. This was the Lord at work. Well, she gave Debbie all of the information needed to pay off the debt. The bank would also call the sheriff's department on Monday to let them know that the debt was paid. I fasted so that I would know who to pay. My Heavenly Father heard my plea. I couldn't say or think enough about my Heavenly Father and my brother Jesus Christ. Mary expressed my feelings the best in Luke 1:46-55 (KJV):

Mary said, "My soul doth magnify the Lord, and my spirit hath rejoiced in God my Savior. For He hath regarded the low estate of His handmaiden; for, behold, from henceforth all generations shall call me blessed. For He that is mighty hath done to me great things; and Holy is His name. And His mercy is on them that fear Him from generation to generation. He hath shewed strength with His arm; He hath scattered the proud in the imagination of their hearts. He hath put down the mighty from their seats, and exalted them of low degree. He hath filled the hungry with good things; and the rich He hath sent empty away. He hath holden His servant Israel, in remembrance of His mercy; As He spake to our fathers, to Abraham, and to his seed forever.

I thanked my dear Heavenly Father for hearing my prayer. Glory to God in the highest. How great thou art! I could barely hold back my tears. I said good night to Debbie and hung up the phone. I hoped that I would sleep that night.

Chapter 14

For nine years, I lived the life that people dreamed of. And now ,I lived in Ferriday, Louisiana. It was not the end of the world, but you could see the end of the world from Ferriday! I opened a computer store using my own money. I earned a great sum of money and didn't have to work. We built a successful MLM business so financially we were doing well. We were in Phoenix, AZ for a training meeting. I was finally going to get to meet one of my favorite speakers. We were sitting in the Phoenix Suns basketball arena and there were about fifteen thousand people here. My favorite football team would be playing in the Super Bowl later that day after the function. So today was a great day. The speaker had just come out to the stage. He began speaking. He was doing a great job and I was learning so much. This happened in January 2000 and I had great plans for my business. I had a very good group of team members here with us. Nothing would stop this team.

My cell phone vibrated. It was my sister so I had to answer. My sister said to me, "We need to talk."

I asked my sister, "Do you mean right now?"

She said, "Yes."

At this time, the cost for a cell phone call was about sixty cents a minute. My sister told me, "Dad is sick and he is about to go into surgery."

I told her, "Let me get to a pay phone and I will call back."

I told Debbie that my Dad was sick and I needed to go and call him. It took me about five minutes to walk up the stairs to a pay phone. I called my sister and asked her, "Why is Dad having surgery done?"

My sister broke down crying and said, "Daddy is dead!"

I said, "This cannot be possible. I just talked to you a few minutes ago." Yet my dad had passed away. My concern quickly turned to my mother. My parents had been married over 60 years and I was sure she would not take this very well. When I turned around from the phone, my team was standing there. I quickly told my team what had happened and that I needed to get a flight home. I asked them to stay for the function, but they told me that if I left they were leaving also.

I spoke with the airlines and they had flight delays everywhere. It appeared there was no way to get a flight. I called back and forth trying to keep everyone up to date as to when I could get there. As I stood in the airport, my mind wondered what would be the outcome of this matter. I tried to eat, but could not. I tried to watch some of the football game. The Rams were playing the Titans for the Super Bowl and I could not watch it. I did see the last drive of the game. The Rams won the Super Bowl but it had very little meaning to me. I finally got a flight to Atlanta. I flew to Atlanta and Debbie flew to New Orleans later that day. From Atlanta, I picked up my niece and drove to Moss Point, Mississippi. This was where my father lived. This was a very tough time for my family. My biggest concern was my mother. She did as well as possible. I spoke with Debbie and told her that I was considering moving to Moss Point to be with my Mom. After burying my Dad, I went back to Louisiana. Considering moving to Moss Point was a very difficult decision for me.

My brother Charles' wife was in the hospital and she was not doing well. Clara was in the hospital in Hattiesburg, MS. I had planned to go to Hattiesburg to see her and then from there back home to see my mom. I decided to move to Moss Point but I had not told Debbie yet. I was feeling so badly for my brother for he had lost his Dad and was about to lose his wife. So I planned to go to Hattiesburg the next day. Now she was much more than a sister-in-law to me. She actually helped raise me. She was more like a mother figure to me. But before I could leave for Hattiesburg, I received a call from Moss Point. My mother had a massive stroke and was in the hospital. This was only ten days after my Dad's funeral. I was told to come home right now for my mom was not going to make it through the night. Debbie and I rushed to Moss Point. It was about a three and half hour drive. When I reached the hospital, the whole family was there except Charles. My mom was on a respirator and the doctor gave her no chance of surviving. I asked, "Has anyone talked to Charles?" I was told that no one called him because they didn't think he could take' much more bad news. I told them that I would call him. When I spoke to Charles, he was suffering greatly after losing his dad and now his wife only had days to live. I told him about Mom and told him that "there was nothing we can do." He said he would come down to Moss Point as soon as possible. Then my sister took the phone and talked to Charles. I went back to my mom's bedside. She was unconscious and had tubes everywhere. I am sure my family prayed for my mom, but praying was not something I did for I knew no God. We were able to get some sleep that night and my mom made it through the night.

The next day was more of the same. The doctors were checking my mom with no hope on their faces. Another day passed and there was no progress for my mom. The doctors told us again that there was not a chance for her to recover. Then we got the word that Clara, my sister-in-law, had passed. We had not even gotten over my Dad passing and now my sister-in-law had passed away! How much can people take before it is too much? Debbie and I went home from the hospital; we were staying at my brother's house. These deaths were wearing the family down. So we all went to bed early that night because the doctors wanted to meet with us the next day. I was sleeping and around 4 am, Debbie and I were awakened by a touch lamp that stood about four feet from the foot of the bed against a wall. Somehow, the lamp just came on without any warning. Debbie and I sat up in the bed. I felt that someone was there in the room with us and I decided to speak to this being. I said, "Dad, if this is you and my mom is with you, make the light brighter." The light became brighter. I looked at Debbie and she looked at me. You must understand I am not one who fears many things so I did not fear what had just happened. I then said, "Dad and Mom, if Nell is with you, make the light brighter." The light actually became even brighter. Debbie and I looked at each other and then looked at the light. And just as it came on, it went out. It was not five minutes later before my brother called me from downstairs saying we needed to get to the hospital. I knew that my mom was in that room that night and my Dad and sister were also there. We got dressed and went to the hospital. The doctors did not think my mom would make it much longer. But they were wrong; she made it through the night. As the day went on, I was in the room holding my mom's hand. The doctor had told all of us that if she moves her hand or fingers it was not because she could hear us. The doctors did not want to give us any false hope. I leaned over to my mom's ear and said these words;

> "Mother, this is your baby. We love you very much. We wished that you could be here with us longer. But I know you love Dad and if you feel it is best to be with him then it is okay for you to leave us. We all will always love you and we will be fine."

I am not sure if Debbie heard what I said to my mom but I know Debbie saw and heard what happened next. I said to my mom, if you can hear me move only your index finger. She moved that one finger. I then ask my mom, "Did you understand what I said? If so move only the finger next to your index finger." And she did. So I kissed her and said goodbye.

Now the doctors wanted to meet with all of the family members. We gathered in a room. The doctors told us they wanted to take my mom off the machine. We all agreed. The doctors told us that my mom would not make it once the machines were removed. We all understood. So they took my mom off life support. And for the next 24 hours, they were surprised that she did not die. We all went home to get some sleep and came back to the hospital the next day. The doctors called us to another conference. They told us the only reason my mom has not passed away is because she wanted to go home. So they released her so that we could take her home. There were a number of things that had to be done to get the house ready for her. We brought our Mom home and the family took care of all the details.

The funeral for my sister-in-law was the next day. I left that morning to go to the funeral. The funeral was in Prentiss, MS. After the funeral, Debbie and I finally headed home for what I hoped was a week. I had planned to come back to Moss Point on the weekend. That did not happen. I got the call on day three that my mother had passed away. Debbie and I got things together and headed to Moss Point for another funeral. I will not write the details of the funeral. But I will touch upon a subject that I have always had a problem with. The preacher at all three funerals stated that my dad, mom and sister-in-law all went to heaven. This concept totally goes against the Bible. Let me discuss this in more detail.

According to the Bible when we die, we do not go to heaven. If we went directly to heaven when we died, then there would not be a need for a judgment day. This would make the Bible wrong. The people who say we go directly to heaven do not understand the Bible. Let us examine what the Bible states happens at our death. When Jesus was on the cross, just minutes before his death, He stated to the person next to him, "Today, you will be with Me in Paradise." Yet to the other man Jesus did not say the same. It appears there is another place that the other man was going upon his death. Notice Jesus never said that today you would be with Me in heaven to anyone. So where did Jesus go? Jesus went to Paradise as He stated. Jesus reveals something interesting while he was in Paradise. Jesus met with the people in this Paradise. The Bible states that there was another place called "Spirit Prison." Jesus did preach to those spirits in prison. Based on the Bible, when we die we will go either to Paradise or Spirit Prison. When Jesus left Paradise and returned to the earth, He met Mary Magdalene. Mary reached out to touch Jesus. Jesus told Mary, 'Touch Me not, for I have not yet ascended to My Father." Here is the question, "Who is Jesus' Father?" Next question, "Where does Jesus' Father live?" If Jesus' Father lives in heaven, then Jesus has not been there yet. At Jesus' death, He did not go to Heaven and neither will we at our death. Here are the scriptures for you to review concerning this matter. (KJV)

Luke 23:42-43

42 And he said unto Jesus, Lord, remember me when thou comest into thy kingdom.
43 And Jesus said unto him, Verily I say unto thee, Today shalt thou be with me in paradise.

1st Peter 3:18-20

18 For Christ also hath once suffered for sins, the just for the unjust, that he might bring us to God, being put to death in the flesh, but quickened by the Spirit:
19 By which also he went and preached unto the spirits in prison;
20 Which sometime were disobedient, when once the long suffering of God waited in the days of Noah, while the ark

was a preparing, wherein few, that is, eight souls were saved by water.

John 20:16-17

16 Jesus saith unto her, Mary. She turned herself, and saith unto him, Rabboni; which is to say, Master.
17 Jesus saith unto her, Touch me not; for I am not yet ascended to my Father: but go to my brethren, and say unto them, I ascend unto my Father, and your Father; and *to* my God, and your God.

I was not a Christian and didn't belong to any church. I really didn't believe I would ever be a Christian nor would I join any church. But, I could read the Bible and understand what it said. And it appeared to me that the Bible states when we die we do not go directly to Heaven!

I lost my dad at the end of January. I lost my sister-in-law in the middle of February. I lost my mom the first of March. All of them were lost in the same year less than 60 days apart. I tell this story to give you an idea of the pain that human beings go though in life. This pain almost destroyed me. Now I asked myself many times where this God was, we needed Him now. My mom knew Him but I did not. I remembered my mom's famous words, "The Lord would not bring more upon you than you could bear." Well this theory was being well tested. I still could not accept Christianity for I saw the corruption within the religion. Plus, if there was a true Christian church then where was it? Jesus was the only person I knew of that claimed to have been born, died, came back to life and never died again. Yet where was He? How would I find him? It appeared to me that no one knew where He was or how to contact Him. If Jesus did exist, He would have to fix the disastrous denomination concept that had destroyed His religion. These deaths were taking a toll on me mentally, physically and financially. I just wanted to pack my belongings and go back to Atlanta. Again, I turned inward to try to protect myself from such great pain. Debbie and I went back to Ferriday.

Chapter 15

Day 11 & 12

I slept very well that night. I prayed most of the night. My cellmate said I talked in my sleep a lot. I didn't remember anything. It was 6:00 in the morning and I was still fasting. I had been reading the Pearl of Great Price. It was a great book. My cellmate was a Navajo Indian. I discussed many things with him. He was a very intelligent man. This was a great opportunity to ask questions to a Navajo Indian. It was interesting that people in jail were very smart. I remembered my father-in-law telling AJ, "Son, there are plenty of smart people in jail." Well, he was right. I asked my cellmate to tell me how did the Indians get to the land we call America. He told me stories that were told to him. The Indians believed they came from South America. He said there was a god that had them move from the south to the north. I asked him, "How far south did the Indians live?" He told me that America was their land, both south and north America. He said that Indians owned all of America until the white people stole the land from them. This was beginning to get interesting when the guard announced breakfast time. We ate breakfast a lot later on this weekend. This was my second weekend and I had four more weekends to be here. I did not believe that the city of Baton Rouge would send someone to Utah to escort me back to Louisiana. I knew Baton Rouge and their only interest was the money. I had to get the people

I owed money to paid and Baton Rouge would release the warrant. I had given my breakfast to by cellmate. He kept food in his drawer for a rainy day.

We were on our break time now. I would not call Debbie this morning. She was working on paying the bank and I did not want to interrupt her. Watching a football game in jail was just not the same. I watched a little of the game and didn't even remember who was playing. A group of us got together to play spades. It was okay but I was just not into it, so I went back into the cell. I was still praying and fasting so that I would get out of here next week no later than Tuesday. I had so many people to pay and no money, business or job. However, if I could just get out of jail, I would do whatever it took to get my debts paid. I estimated that from the time I left jail it would take 30 days to stabilize my personal finances. Then I could pay all of the business debt. As of now, I had not spent any of the five thousand I borrowed. If I could get by without spending it then my 30 day financial recovery plan would be intact.

I called Debbie to get an update. I talked with Debbie; she could not send the check today. The bank could not give her a cashiers check. Debbie would have to pick up the cashier check on Monday and the bank would get it Tuesday. Debbie was working hard and I thought she was doing much better. I would fast tonight and pray for her for she is the only mortal person that could help me now. As always, Debbie would rise to the occasion. I would not give up on the Lord. I know He would not give up on me. I continued to read Doctrine and Covenants until the lights went out at 11 pm.

Day 12

It was a night like few I have had. It was very hard to sleep. I woke up at 1:30 and 3:30 and 5:30. I wasn't sure why. I was tired last night yet I could not sleep. I told Debbie yesterday I would not call her this morning. I got up, ended my fast and ate breakfast. Then we cleaned the room and I got so tired. I just went back to sleep until 9 am. The guard let us out of our cell around 10 am. I worked out some and took a shower. I wanted so badly to call Debbie, but I did not. I went back to my cell. I partook of the Sacrament. It was great. I read some of the Book of Mormon: 1 Nephi chapters 11 and 12. I awaited the week so that I would see the power of the Lord work wonders in my life. I began to think about the six questions that had always kept me from being a Christian growing up. Those six things or questions were:

(1) According to the Bible, people who are called by God should not be paid to preach His gospel, which God gave to them freely.
(2) How does one identify the Holy Ghost?
(3) If the Temple was so importance in the Bible, then where is the Temple today?
(4) Why is there not a Prophet today?
(5) The Trinity, as explained, is not possible.
(6) What happens to the dead that have never heard the gospel?

It was time to go to church. I talked with my cellmate, Steve. He decided to go to church with me.

The brother who conducted the service did a great job. The focus of the lesson was forgiveness and Jesus being our brother. I spoke in church about the guys in lockup with me. These guys were some of the best people I had ever met. Steve gave the closing prayer in his native Navajo language. Even though we did not know the Navajo tongue, God knew all tongues. But to edify us, Steve translated the prayer to English so that we could understand. This is an example of why someone speaking in tongues is useless unless there is an interpreter to translate the tongues. There was not a dry eye in this room of about fifty men. This is an example of speaking in tongues. Speaking in tongues, should not be used unless there is someone there who can translate the tongues.

See 1 Corinthians 14:2-6

2 For he that speaketh in an unknown tongue speaketh not unto men, but unto God: for no man understandeth him; howbeit in the spirit he speaketh mysteries.
3 But he that prophesieth speaketh unto men to edification, and exhortation, and comfort.
4 He that speaketh in an unknown tongue edifieth himself; but he that prophesieth edifieth the church.
5 I would that ye all spake with tongues, but rather that ye prophesied: for greater is he that prophesieth than he that speaketh with tongues, except he interpret, that the church may receive edifying.
6 Now, brethren, if I come unto you speaking with tongues, what shall I profit you, except I shall speak to you either by revelation, or by knowledge, or by prophesying, or by doctrine?

Read these scriptures. Should you not understand, pray to your Heavenly Father and He will reveal understanding to you.

Church was over and we were headed back to our cells. It appeared that we were on lockdown. This occurred when there were not enough guards to watch all the prisoners in the jail complex. The guard rushed us to our cells. I prayed that this was not true for that meant that I would not be able to talk to Debbie. We ate dinner and waited to see if we were on lockdown or not. We were good because lockdown was over. That was almost five hours in the cells. I would get to call Debbie.

I spoke with Debbie. Things looked better. A friend of ours, who is a judge, was reviewing my case. I thanked God for being my Father and my friend. I would continue my fasting and praying. I thanked God for Debbie and all the members of my church family. I could go to bed with some good news. Tomorrow was Monday. I was happy because the courts would be open. Maybe we could find out who I owe. Then we could find a way for me to get me out of jail. I said goodnight.

Chapter 16

There I owned a computer store. It was a lot of work running the store. One day while I was at the store, there was a problem with the accounting books. Debbie was my bookkeeper, so I called her to come down and help. Debbie said when she was coming out of our front door, there were two young girls there about to knock on our door. Debbie said, "How can I help you?"

The young ladies asked, "Would you be interested in listening to some information about Jesus Christ?"

Debbie said, "Yes, I would, it would be fine, but I cannot do it right now I have got to go help my husband."

The young ladies asked, "Well, can we get your number and we will call you to set up an appointment to come by later?" Debbie gave them the number and they said that they would call back.

I did not know anything about this, but one night about two weeks later, we were sitting at home when the phone rang. Debbie picked up the phone and said to me, "There are some missionaries on the phone who would like to come by and talk to us about their church."

I said "Really? Debbie, ask them if they are Jehovah Witnesses?" So she asked them and they said no. So I told Debbie to ask them, "Are they Seven Day Adventist?"

They said no.

I said, "Well ask them what church are they from?"

Debbie asked them. Then Debbie came back to me and said, "They said they are from The Church of Jesus Christ of Latter Day Saints." Then I said to Debbie, "I have heard of that church many years ago. I do not really know anything about it so tell them to come by for a visit. I would like to meet with them." I left it at that and Debbie set up a time and told me what time I needed to be home for these people to come by.

About two months before this night, Debbie told me the most shocking thing that I had ever heard from her. She said, "AJ is getting older now and I want him raised in the church. Since he is a boy, he needs to see you go to church as an example."

I did not say a word but I thought "What? I am not going to church! Why would I want to go to church? Those people are nothing but crooks and they sell the gospel to people to feed their lifestyle. They rip people off and they convince them about all of this religious stuff and then take their money."

After I had this conversation in my head, I replied, "Debbie I just cannot do this. I cannot go to church. "

Debbie replied, "But I want him raised in the church."

I resisted again by telling her that I was not even sure I believed in Jesus Christ. Well, when your wife says things a certain way you know she means it. So I knew she meant what she was saying. I said, "Okay, I will go to church... as long as I can pick the church we attend." This concept was very difficult for me. I totally did not want to do this because I did not want to be part of this Christian craziness. I believed the whole concept of church in today's society was a racket. It was a money making machine for people that did not want to get an honest job. I looked at Christianity that way.

We began to attend different churches as I searched for one that I could tolerate. I do not know how many churches we attended. Maybe twenty-five or thirty, I do not know. Some of the churches we went in, I would immediately turn right around and walk out. Some of the churches, we would sit through the whole program. I would think about how the things these preachers were preaching did not match the words that were in the Bible. What I saw and heard in these churches was not based on the concepts or the writings that were in the Bible. Oh, I understood the concept of what these preachers were doing.

The concept was this: the music was played loudly to generate emotions within the people. Once the people became emotional due to the music, the ministers would claim this emotional feeling was the Holy Ghost. Ironically, this same emotional excitement was generated no matter what music you listened to. Selling religion was such a big racket. Ripping people off was what this really was. I just did not want to be a part of this blatant fleecing of the people in the name of religion. I felt if there were a God, he would never approve of these actions. I always felt the church members were good people. The church members were doing the best they could. But the corrupt ministers were leading the members nowhere and taking their money at the same time. As you can tell, I did not have good feelings concerning ministers and preachers. So we just kept going to different churches. I had made a list of ten churches by this time. I was not getting close to joining any of them. Yet somehow, I was going to pick the least terrible one of the churches on my list. I was just trying to buy time and hope that Debbie would forget about this, but she did not. She was serious about this. I knew I was going to have to find a church!

Then the day came that the missionaries were to come to our home. I had not met them yet. There was a knock on the door. I opened the door and saw these two little girls standing there. The little girls said, "We are missionaries from The Church of Jesus Christ of Latter Day Saints." And I thought, really? I mean you cannot be here to talk to me about religion. I probably know twenty times more about your Bible than you do. But I was being polite so I let them in and they came inside. We went over to the kitchen table and the little girls sat down. They had these little nametags on their dress. One of the nametags read Sister Finch and the other Sister Pickett. I did not think much about these little girls, but they were cute.

We sat at the table and they began to talk. They were talking about faith and repentance. You know, the same run down that all religious people talk about. I really was not listening to what they were saying. They continued to talk about Jesus Christ. Oh my gracious, I thought, I really do not want to hear anything about Jesus Christ. However, I had promised Debbie I would be nice and I had to see it through. So I had to give them a chance. So they went on and talked about many, many things. I already knew most of the things these missionaries were speaking about. I really had little to no interest in this thing for I had rejected these concepts many years ago. But then they began to tell a story. This was the first time that they really caught my attention. They were talking about a young man named Joseph Smith. They said that this young man was trying to decide which church to join. He had been to many churches and he did not know which one to join. This young man became confused concerning Christianity. He was not sure which denomination was the correct one. He began to think that maybe he should ask God which church to join. This story really caught my attention. You see, I knew this story. This was my story. I had already lived this story. Somehow, these two young girls were telling my story, but their story was about Joseph Smith. Joseph and I shared the exact same story. What were the chances of this happening to someone else! It intrigued me because I wanted to see what would happen at the end of Joseph's story. I was sure that his story would end just like my story.

The missionaries continued to talk about Joseph growing up. Then they mentioned a scripture in James and mentioned that Joseph decided to go to a grove of trees to pray to God. Joseph wanted God to tell him which church to join. I thought, really? You see, some twenty years earlier I had done the same thing that Joseph Smith was about to do. I was very intrigued by this story. The missionaries continued, "When Joseph reached the grove of trees, he knelt down to pray to God concerning his issue about which church to join." Honestly, I already knew the rest of the story before they even told it. I knew that Joseph was going to kneel down and pray. He was going to ask God and Jesus some questions (prayer). Then nothing was going to happen because I had already tried this concept. The missionaries stated Joseph prayed and then he stated, "I saw a pillar of light exactly over my head, above the brightness of the sun, which descended gradually until it fell upon me. When the light rested upon me, I saw two Personages, whose brightness and glory defy all description, standing above me in the air. One of them spake unto me, calling me by name and said, pointing to the other, This is My Beloved Son. Hear Him!"

Joseph stated he saw Heavenly Father and Jesus Christ. When the missionaries finish this statement, I stated "What? You are telling me that Joseph saw Heavenly Father and Jesus Christ?" The missionaries responded, "Yes." I said to myself, not to them, "It is about doggone time Jesus Christ and Heavenly Father showed up." I was getting really concerned that they did not exist at all because nobody had seen them. So all of a sudden, here is this boy Joseph Smith who saw them. I had no problem believing the story because I had tried the same thing. I had already decided that the only person who could fix this Christian denomination mess was the one who created the original Christian religion. It made sense to me that God himself would come to fix it.

It was a great story and I knew I would have to study Joseph Smith to try to understand who he was and what God told him. I wanted to know because God did not tell me anything. But maybe He told Joseph Smith something. As I began to focus on the idea of studying Joseph, I noticed the book the missionaries had on the table. It was a little blue, maybe black, book and they would push it toward me and then pull it back. Again, they would push this book toward me and then pull it back. I could see the title that said, "Another Testament of Jesus Christ?" I wondered where that book came from. Now you have to remember that I already had two books that contained a testament of Jesus Christ. These were the Holy Bible and the Quran. So here I was looking at a third book concerning this Jesus Christ character. So I wanted that book. I mean I really wanted that book. Now I will tell you that the book was The Book of Mormon. I kept thinking how much they would charge me for that book. I was ready to offer up to $40 for the book because I had to have it. This was the first time I had even heard of the Book of Mormon.

All of a sudden, the missionaries said, "We're going to leave this book with you."

And I said, "No, no, no, you do not have to leave it with me because I will pay you for the book."

The missionaries stated, "No, we leave the Book of Mormon with people for them to study."

And I said, "No, no, no, I cannot take your book without paying you." You see, my life was based on money and I understood that a book cost money. I did not want to take that book because if I get "something for nothing," then that meant that there was someone somewhere who was getting "nothing for something." I told the missionaries, "No, I do not want to take the book."

They persisted and said, "We are going to leave the Book of Mormon and some scriptures for you to read. We would like for you to read these scriptures and then we will get back together in three days." Since these missionaries were so persistent, I agreed to take their Book of Mormon. I felt that in three days I could buy the book or give it back to them. Debbie wrote down the appointment.

So everything was fine and this meeting was going to end on a good note. Then the missionaries made a big mistake before leaving. They asked me a question that they should not have asked. I have been asked this question before from many Christians. Every time a Christian would ask me this question and I would answer the question, those Christians would act as if they wanted to take me out back and shoot me. Christians hated me for my answer. So you can understand why I did not want these missionaries to ask this question. But one of the missionaries asked me, "Who do you think Jesus Christ is?" I remember pausing. I picked up the Bible and I picked up their Book of Mormon. I said, "Now according to your books," because I would never claim the Bible or the Book of Mormon as my books, "Jesus is my brother." I waited to see what the missionaries were going to say because I knew they were going to do what the Jehovah Witnesses did. The Jehovah Witness ran from me and they never talked to me again. I felt the missionaries were going to do as other people did and call me an atheist, a devil worshipper, blasphemer and all kinds of mean things.

The two girls (missionaries) looked at each other, smiled and said, "You are right."

I was shocked at their response! I thought, yeah, sure I am correct. I felt this new church might be the worst I had ever met because their missionaries were going to agree with me just to get me to join their church. I felt this was about tithing money. I felt this church just was in it for the money just like most of the other Christian churches. I just thought, yeah, sure you believe me. I could hardly wait for them to leave. I really wanted them to leave because they had an advantage over me because they knew about a book that I did not know about. Then they had the nerve to pick certain scriptures out of that book that they wanted me to read. When they finally left, I knew I only had three days before they were going to come back. So I told Debbie, "There is no way we are going to read those scriptures that they told us to read. This is how the game is played. They are trying to set us up, but that is not going to work. This is what we are going to do. I am going to read the whole book and when they come back I am going to know just as much as they do so that I can be on their level."

Chapter 17

Day 13

did not sleep very much last night. It was Monday and there was hope of some good things happening this week. This was why I did not sleep well. First, I woke up at 1 am and prayed to my Lord for sleep to come. I did fall asleep. I slept from about 2 am until 5 am. Then the normal 5:30 ritual took place: get out of bed; stand by the door to be counted. Then I watched the guys who needed medicine get released from their cell to get their medicine. I waited for breakfast and to break my fast. I prayed deeply that things would go just as my fast had. In Jesus' name, I prayed, Amen.

Breakfast was served. We got to leave our cell and go downstairs to get our food. We then brought the food back to our room to eat it. I gave most of my food to Steve. He stored this food for a rainy day. The food was not too bad. You learned to eat what you had. Debbie's food would have tasted so good right then. Breakfast was over and we had just finished cleaning our cell. It would be about three hours before they would allow us out of our cell. So I went to sleep. I had been sleeping for the last hour. The bottom group of guys were out of their cells for their break. I saw two guys get out of jail that day. I was happy for them and awaited my time to leave. I had been thinking about what I would have to do to try to get my life back together once I was out of there. I awaited the challenge and would need to move very quickly. We had lost so much, yet there were so many opportunities. I would be so grateful to the Lord for just giving me the chance. I was reading 1 Nephi Chapter 19 in the Book of Mormon. The Lord spoke to my mind and said, "Call Debbie and have her fax a copy of the check used to pay off the bank and also FedEx a copy of the check to Mary at the bank. Then have Debbie ask Mary to speak to the sheriff to let them know that the debt has been paid." We were let out of our cells. I was trying to get to the phone to call Debbie. I truly needed an update and hoped for progress. I spoke with Debbie. She had sent the money to Mary at the bank. Debbie sent the check overnight so that it would be in Mary's hands by noon tomorrow. Then Mary would call the sheriff and the city of Baton Rouge and there would be no other outstanding items against me from the bank. I gave Debbie the words the Spirit gave to me concerning faxing the information. Debbie said she would fax a copy of the check to Mary. Now it was in the Lord's hands. Now I would have to wait until tonight to call Debbie again to see how things were going. We had done all that the Lord directed us to do, Amen.

Steve and I began discussing scriptures. He wanted to know more and I answered every question he asked. I gave him many scriptures to read in the Bible and in the Book of Mormon. I had been focusing on the following scriptures myself. 1 Nephi 22:23/ 2 Nephi 1:6; 21:22-29; 2 Nephi 3:11-12 in the Book of Mormon. I continued to pray to the Lord concerning my fast and prayers so that I would get out of jail tomorrow and go home to Debbie. How great it would be to leave this place and go home. I added one more item to my covenant. This was to start a journal and write my history in that journal. Oh Father, I prayed, please make it possible for me to go home tomorrow, Amen.

I was out of my cell again and I called Debbie to get an update. Debbie faxed the check to Mary but could not get her on the phone.

Debbie was able to reach my lawyer and she sent him all of the papers concerning my case. Things were happening just as in the vision. Roy, my lawyer, was the one who was supposed to get me out of here. Now, things were going exactly that way since we were finally in contact with him. I would continue my fast at 1800 hours and pray to my God, Amen. I was so humble right now. What could I say? The Lord was in full control. I was just amazed. I could hardly speak. The same as Nephi when the Lord did exactly as he stated and Nephi watched it all happen. The time was near. September 9th I would be released from Utah County jail to go home and be with my wife. I would have to start anew to keep the covenants that I had made with my Heavenly Father. I would sleep in peace tonight and fast and pray to my Heavenly Father throughout the night any time I was awake. I would continue to pray for my release tomorrow. I would pray for my family. I would pray for everyone. Then I would pray that my Heavenly Father would open my heart and mind to guide me in what I needed to do concerning a job and my business. How would I proceed to take care of my family? How would I stand with the church? How would I stand with my children and grandchildren? There was so much work to do. I asked Heavenly Father to give me the strength in body and mind to go do as the spirit directed me to do. I asked Him to show me the path I must take and give me the wisdom to do all that I had covenanted to do. 2 Nephi 28-29 (Book of Mormon). I talked to Debbie. She was well. We were hoping to get out of here tomorrow. I was fasting and praying. Another night was coming and I was going to sleep very well.

Chapter 18

For three straight days I read nothing but the Book of Mormon. I read it at my office; I read it at my store; I read it at night; I read it in the morning and in three days, I had finished the whole book. I was ready now. I knew their Book of Mormon characters and stories. In the Bible, you have characters like Moses, Abraham, Joshua, Jesus Christ, John the Baptist and David and Goliath. So after I read the Book of Mormon I knew Lehi and Nephi. I knew all of those Book of Mormon people and I was ready to meet with the missionaries. A word of thought, "How can a person make a decision about something that they have not studied?"

When the missionaries came back to our home after three days, I was ready for them. They came into the house. Their first question was, "Well, did you read the scriptures that we asked you to read?"

I said, "Well ok, I will admit it, I read the whole Book of Mormon."

The missionaries looked at each other in disbelief. I was sure they did not expect me to read the complete Book of Mormon in three days. My thought was, "You think you all are just going to come here and run roughshod over me with a book that I have never seen before? That is not going to happen. I am prepared. Now we can discuss things."

The missionary asked me, "Well, do you think the Book of Mormon is true?"

I said, "Well, let me tell you this." I picked up the Bible and said, "Do you see this book? This is a good book, but I do not believe this Book." Then I picked up the Book of Mormon and said, "Now you see, this book? This book is just like the Bible. The principles are identical. So, of course, I do not believe the Book of Mormon. Basically what we have here are two books that I do not believe, but we are going to work on this because maybe there is something in these two books that I can learn. So let's start from this point and see what happens." We started from that point and the missionaries began the second lesson.

This second lesson was about the Holy Ghost. I remember that we were sitting there and missionaries began to talk about the Holy Ghost. The missionaries began to explain to me how to identify the Holy Ghost. Now, here is the key to something the missionaries did not know. No one knew of my questions concerning Christianity. One of my six questions was how do you identify the Holy Ghost. Guess what the missionaries wanted to discuss, "How you identify the Holy Ghost?" I did not know at the time, but the Lord knew exactly where to start with me. So, we went through this lesson. The missionaries taught me how to identify the Holy Ghost by a still small voice. When they said that, I knew that it matched what was in the Bible. I thought, "That is pretty good that they knew about the Holy Ghost. So I asked them a question, "So what do you think about speaking in tongues?"

The missionaries stated, "Speaking in tongues is basically when you are speaking the language of someone else." And I thought hmm really? These girls were pretty sharp because that was true based on the Bible. Not based on what I know, but based on what I read in the Bible. So at least they were matching the Bible. Which I thought was awesome, since others just made up things that were not in the Bible.

The missionaries continued talking about the Holy Ghost. I was really impressed with them and the things they had to say. What they did not know is that I had spoken with many Christian leaders concerning identifying the Holy Ghost. Following is a summary of what these Christian leaders had to say about the Holy Ghost and the concept of speaking in tongues.

1. First, the Holy Ghost comes upon people or a person "catches" the Holy Ghost. When this process occurs a person will:

    a. Begin to jump and dance in an uncontrollable fashion. The term is called "shouting." I have seen many people shouting in many different fashions. Yet I have not been able to find in the Bible anything about a person shouting when visited by the Holy Ghost. Most Christian denominations use the day of Pentecost (Acts Chapter 2) scripture to explain the concept of shouting. But if you read this scripture, you will not find the concept of shouting contained within this scripture. So where does this concept come from?

    b. Then there are some denominations that believe that the Holy Ghost is identified by what they call "speaking in tongues." The concept of "speaking in tongues" refers to the Holy Ghost coming upon someone and the person beginning to speak a new language. This new language is supposed to be a language that can only be understood by God. When I asked Christian leaders about this concept and where in the Bible this concept existed, they sent me back to the day of Pentecost (Acts Chapter 2). When you read this scripture, the concept of "speaking in tongues" as an indication that the Holy Ghost has visited someone is just not there. The Disciples did speak in a tongue so that everyone who was at the location understood the message in their native tongue. This was not a language that only God understood! In fact, the Disciples spoke only in

Hebrew. The Holy Ghost made it possible for the Hebrew language to be heard in the native tongue of the individuals who did not speak Hebrew. What would be the use of someone speaking the Gospel in a language that no one understands? Jesus never did, nor did any Christian or Jewish leader in the Bible. (Please read 1 Corinthians 14)

After about an hour, the missionaries had completed another session. One of the Sisters stated, "Well, we want to set up another appointment to come back again and talk to you some more about the Gospel."

I said "Really? Ok, fine, you can come back." The appointment was set for three days later.

Sister Pickett was a pretty sharp young lady. She began to realize that I knew a lot about Christianity. The next time the missionaries came to my house, they took a different approach. I don't know if they came up with this new approach on their own or not, yet I sensed the new approach. The approach was to ask me a question about the subject they were to teach. This way they could find out my thoughts first and then teach the lesson based on my knowledge level. This way they could figure out how to teach me. Sister Finch was more of a studier. She studied you and listened very closely to your response. Sister Pickett was the talker. So Sister Pickett and I hit it off immediately. I mean we were kindred spirits. We just kind of knew each other somehow.

The three days were up and I wondered what they planned to teach this time. There was a knock at the door and Debbie answered the door. The missionaries came in and we sat at the table to begin our study. A prayer was given. Sister Pickett asked me, "Why do you think that there are so many different Christian churches?" Little did they know I had already studied this concept over the years. I had given a lot of thought to this matter. I remember saying to them, "This is why there are so many different churches or denominations of Christianity. It appears no one knows exactly what is right or how the gospel should be taught. So what has happened is that once there was one denomination or church. The church had all of the principles of the gospel. Then someone decided that the concept of baptism was more important than the rest of the principles. So the group of people who believed that baptism was the most important thing left the church and created their own church. This created a second church or denomination. Therefore, this process continued to happen because no one knew all of the principals of Jesus Christ's Church. These breakoffs continued to happen and multiple churches or denominations were created. All of these denominations are trying to serve God using the same Bible, but because of their interpretation they created multiple churches."

They listened to what I said and then stated, "That is good. We are glad you understand that, but let's talk about how the original Church was setup by Jesus Christ."

I thought that this was interesting. You see, I never thought about what the original Church would look like, how it was setup by Jesus Christ. The missionaries begin to teach us as to how the original Church was setup by Jesus Christ. They used these cups to lay out the foundation of the church. First, there was Jesus Christ. Then there were the apostles who were represented by twelve cups. The missionaries then setup these twelve cups, which represented the twelve apostles on the table. On top of these apostles' cups, the Sisters stacked cups that represented principles of the gospel. These principles were faith, baptism, prayer and other principles that govern Jesus' church. As they stacked these cups of principles, they placed Jesus Christ at the top of this pyramid. The church was built with Jesus Christ as the head of the church. All of the principles of the gospel were next in the stack. The apostles were the bottom part of the stack. When Jesus was killed, He went off to Heaven and they showed how through revelation via the Holy Ghost, Jesus revealed his will to the apostles. Through revelation to his apostles, Jesus guided his church. The missionaries then asked, "What would happen if the apostles were killed?" The twelve cups (apostles) on the bottom maintained this concept of Jesus' Church. The missionaries began to remove a cup (apostle) as each one was killed. Very quickly, I realized that this church was not going to stand much longer. All of a sudden, the whole church just crumbled. I looked at this concept and I said, "That is exactly what happened." See I had already known what happened but I had never seen it illustrated like this. It was the greatest illustration that they could have shown me. This made me consider the possibility that Jesus could be real! I thought, "This is exactly why we have all of these different denominations today. The apostles were dead and then no one knew exactly how the church should be run." The missionaries left that night. They had truly caught my attention. I considered for the first time that Christianity could be true. I knew I had to study Christianity more and understand how the Sisters knew this information. I began to focus on the relationship between the Bible and the Book of Mormon. I really began to study these two books. These two books claimed the same things, that Jesus was the Son of God. I did not believe in either book, yet these two books contained the exact same principals. I just kept thinking, "How is it possible that now I have three witnesses that Jesus Christ is someone special." Now my focus turned to understanding who or what this person Jesus Christ was.

I began to tie the timing of the Bible and the Book of Mormon together. I tested the principles of the gospel in both books. I studied the Jesus of both books. After studying these two books, I could not deny that they were identical. Now my task was to prove that both books were not true. My next five days were filled with massive studying of two books that testified of Jesus Christ. I knew that if I could break one of the books, then the other would fall also. I searched for any principal or teaching that would be different in the books. There were not any cracks in the book's relationship. Heavenly Father and Jesus Christ were the same in both books! In fact, the Book of Mormon provided great support to the Bible.

When the missionaries came back to our home, it began again with a knock on the door. I was very much prepared to break the missionaries. I had to prove that the Bible and the Book of Mormon were not true. Neither the missionaries nor Debbie knew of the six things that I wrote when I was nineteen years old that came back to my memory. So many times, I had broken Christians of all denominations with their inability to answer any of the six things. Yet these missionaries had already answered two of the six questions. Up until this point, no one had answered any of the questions. However, I knew these Sisters could not answer all six questions. I knew that I was going to get an opportunity to ask those other questions. Once the missionaries couldn't answer them, then I was going to say, "Your church is just like all other Christian churches."

The missionaries began focusing on the concept of a restored gospel. They asked me, "Who do you think could restore the gospel if the gospel was messed up?" They used my words. I always said the Gospel was messed up and could not be fixed. I said, "Well, it would have to be the originators, the people who created it. That is who would have to fix the gospel." Therefore, they began to talk about how Jesus' church was restored through the Prophet Joseph Smith. I understood this concept of a prophet. I knew that if God were going to restore his Gospel, He would not do it Himself. I knew God would use a man, because when Moses lead the Israelites out of Egypt in reality God restored the gospel through Moses. And if you think about it, who came to see Moses? "The Lord, Himself." Why? "Because He needed to fix His people." And so who came to see Joseph Smith? "The Lord Himself." Why? "Because He needed to fix His people." I understood this concept and it was a great concept. The missionaries went through the whole thing about how the gospel was restored through Joseph Smith. I thought to myself that this was great, but I still didn't believe this stuff. I thought, you (missionaries) are sounding great, but there are still four things you have not answered yet." Surely, if God restored His gospel, He might reveal the answer to my questions. I had not asked the missionaries my questions yet, but they answered another one without even knowing it.

As we went through the story of how the gospel was restored, I knew this concept could be true. I knew the first step to there being a true Christian church must begin with the Gospel being restored. I knew the gospel could not be restored by any rewrite of the Bible or by new versions of the Bible. It could only be restored by God. There are three scriptures I will reference here that bear witness that the gospel must be restored.

Acts 3:19-21 (KJV)

19 ¶ Repent ye therefore, and be converted, that your sins may be blotted out, when the times of refreshing shall come from the presence of the Lord;
20 And he shall send Jesus Christ, which before was preached unto you:
21 Whom the heaven must receive until the times of restitution of all things, which God hath spoken by the mouth of all his holy prophets since the world began.

What is this refreshing that Peter is speaking about? This statement was made not long after Jesus' death. If Jesus left the fullness of His gospel on earth at His death, then why would this gospel need to be refreshed? Why would this gospel need to have a "times of restitution of all things?" It appears that something would happen to the gospel and Jesus would have to refresh (restore) His gospel at some point in the future. Study this scripture for yourself and ask God what it means.

2 THESSALONIANS 2:3 (KJV)

3 Let no man deceive you by any means: for *that day shall not come,* except there come a falling away first, and that man of sin be revealed, the son of perdition;

Here Paul had to calm the people of Thessalonica, for they thought that the end of time was near. Paul told the people that the end of time would not come "except there come a falling away first." What is this "falling away?" If there were a "falling away," would this imply that some type of refreshing would be needed to correct this "falling away?"

Revelation 14:6

6 And I saw another angel fly in the midst of heaven, having the everlasting gospel to preach unto them that dwell on the earth, and to every nation, and kindred, and tongue, and people,

Here John speaks of a vision he had of an "angel...having the everlasting gospel." What is this "everlasting gospel" that the angel is carrying? Is it possible that this "everlasting gospel" is the restored gospel? Could this "everlasting gospel" be the "refreshing" that Peter spoke about? I ask you now to study all of these scriptures and gain an understanding of their meanings.

I propose a question here. Is the Bible true? If the Bible is true, then we must conclude that Peter, Paul and John are telling the truth. For if they are not telling the truth, then the Bible cannot be true. However, if the Bible is true, then Peter, Paul and John are telling the truth. This truth implies that the Gospel of Jesus Christ must be lost! Then, at some point in the future, the Gospel of Jesus Christ will be "restored". If the Gospel of Jesus Christ is to be "restored," then no

Christian denomination can have the full Gospel of Jesus Christ. For if any Christian denomination says they have the full Gospel of Jesus Christ, then they would have the answer to John's prophesies. They must have witnessed the full Gospel of Jesus Christ (the everlasting gospel) being brought to the earth by an angel. For if a church proclaim to have the full gospel and not claim the angel brought the gospel to them, then that church says that John is a liar and the Bible is false.

This was another great meeting with the missionaries. They had no idea of my thoughts concerning the restored gospel. Yet the missionaries did a great job of discussing the gospel "being restored" through Joseph Smith. I became very interested in studying more about the possibility of the Church of Jesus Christ of Latter Day Saints having the "restored" Gospel of Jesus Christ. Yet I still did not believe the Bible or the Book of Mormon, and surely, I did not believe in Jesus Christ. Yet I was moving in the right direction for once in my life.

Chapter 19

Day 14

It was another long night. I got very little sleep. I have been fasting and praying all night. It was morning. Today was the same as yesterday: wake up at 5:00 am, get out of bed and stand at the door of the cell to be counted due to a guard shift change. After being counted, I lay back in the bed for about an hour until it was time for breakfast. I finished eating breakfast and cleaning my cell. Cleaning the cell included cleaning the toilet, washing down the metal mirror, making the bed and sweeping the floor. I thought, man, how do these people put up with this for so long? I saw people get out of jail and then come back three to five days later. My cellmate was beginning to ask more questions about the Book of Mormon. Steve asked, "Does the book of Mormon actually talk about the American Indians?" I told him yes. Steve asked me, "Why would this book even care about the Indians?" I told him this was one of the main reasons I was so impressed with the book. Think about this for a moment, "What white man, in the early 1800s, would write a book that elevates an Indian above himself?" Even to this day, no people would say that another people are actually God's chosen people over his own race. Steve stopped for a moment. I could see in his eyes that his mind was being enlightened by the Holy Ghost. Steve said, "I never thought of it that way." He began to tell me how much he disliked what the white people had done to his people. There were stories from his youth concerning how the Indians had a country that was taken away from them by white people. Steve was beginning to become angry. He talked about how his people tried to help white people and how their kindness was misused. I did not know that there were so many stories in the Navajo's history that had been passed down through the generations. I heard about a proud people from Steve. I asked Steve, "Do you know of any white people who would say that an Indian is a chosen person of God?" The Holy Spirit touched him this time. Steve stood there for about a minute in complete silence. He finally said, "I want to read the Book of Mormon." There it was. That was the Holy Ghost! He touched the heart of Steve and testified to Steve that he needed to read the Book of Mormon. There was no shouting, no speaking in tongues, just a still small voice. See 1st Kings 19:11-12 (KJV). There was no more for me to say. Steve began reading the Book of Mormon.

I climbed up into my bed in the top bunk to wait another two hours before we would be let out of the cell. I was rehearsing my conversion story in my mind. I always reviewed my conversion story about three to four times a month. I did not want to forget what happened to me. I wanted to remember the feelings I had at that time. I wanted to remember when the Holy Ghost enlightened my mind to the understanding of God. I wanted to remember everything I did to not become a member of any Christian Church. I wanted to remember how the Lord touched me both logically and spiritually. I never thought that I would believe the Bible to be true or believe in Jesus Christ. But it was not a preacher, minister or pope of one the many Christian denominations that showed me the way. There were two books that brought to my heart the true meaning of Heavenly Father and Jesus Christ. First, the Quran set my feet on the right path to understanding Christianity. If you take away the Quran, I would have never been what we call a Christian. The second book, which moved me down the road of believing in Heavenly Father and His Son, Jesus

Christ, was the Book of Mormon. This book taught me the most about Heavenly Father and Jesus Christ and their purpose for mankind. The Book of Mormon brought to me an understanding and belief in the Holy Bible. Christians do not seem to understand that the New Testament is a series of books that were added to the Jewish scriptures (Old Testament), making what we call the Holy Bible today. The Jews did not accept the Christians wanting to add the New Testament to their scriptures. Now, today, those same Christians cannot accept that the Book of Mormon is an addition to the Jewish scripture (Old Testament), and an addition to the Christian's scriptures (New Testament).

We were being let out of our cell. Thank God! I had been praying for my family all day. I was also praying for the judges in Louisiana and in Utah that they could find a way to let me out of jail. There was nothing else I could do other than pray for the people who were involved that the Lord would touch their hearts to show me favor. As I sat reading 3rd Nephi in the Book of Mormon, concerning the wonders and teachings of Jesus Christ to the Nephites, I thought of how great the things He showed them. These scriptures should be read again and again for they are so great. They showed me how much Jesus loves us and how much he wants to help us. These were some of the words of Jesus when he visited the land we now call America.

3 Nephi 18:20-22

20 And whatsoever ye shall ask the Father in my name, which is right, believing that ye shall receive, behold it shall be given unto you.

21 Pray in your families unto the Father, always in my name, that your wives and your children may be blessed.

22 And behold, ye shall meet together oft; and ye shall not forbid any man from coming unto you when ye shall meet together, but suffer them that they may come unto you and forbid them not;

3 Nephi 19:4

4 And it came to pass that on the morrow, when the multitude was gathered together, behold, Nephi and his brother whom he had raised from the dead, whose name was Timothy, and also his son, whose name was Jonas, and also Mathoni, and Mathonihah, his brother, and Kumen, and Kumenonhi, and Jeremiah, and Shemnon, and Jonas, and Zedekiah, and Isaiah—now these were the names of the disciples whom Jesus had chosen—and it came to pass that they went forth and stood in the midst of the multitude.

3 Nephi 21:1-3

1 And verily I say unto you, I give unto you a sign, that ye may know the time when these things shall be about to take place—that I shall gather in, from their long dispersion, my people, O house of Israel, and shall establish again among them my Zion;

2 And behold, this is the thing which I will give unto you for a sign—for verily I say unto you that when these things which I declare unto you, and which I shall declare unto you hereafter of myself, and by the power of the Holy Ghost which shall be given unto you of the Father, shall be made known unto the Gentiles that they may know concerning this people who are a remnant of the house of Jacob, and concerning this my people who shall be scattered by them;

3 Verily, verily, I say unto you, when these things shall be made known unto them of the Father, and shall come forth of the Father, from them unto you;

3 Nephi 26: 7-9

7 But behold the plates of Nephi do contain the more part of the things which he taught the people.

8 And these things have I written, which are a lesser part of the things which he taught the people; and I have written them to the intent that they may be brought again unto this people, from the Gentiles, according to the words which Jesus hath spoken.

9 And when they shall have received this, which is expedient that they should have first, to try their faith, and if it shall so be that they shall believe these things then shall the greater things be made manifest unto them.

3 Nephi 27: 2-7

2 And Jesus again showed himself unto them, for they were praying unto the Father in his name; and Jesus came and stood in the midst of them, and said unto them: What will ye that I shall give unto you?

3 And they said unto him: Lord, we will that thou wouldst tell us the name whereby we shall call this church; for there are disputations among the people concerning this matter.

4 And the Lord said unto them: Verily, verily, I say unto you, why is it that the people should murmur and dispute because of this thing?

5 Have they not read the scriptures, which say ye must take upon you the name of Christ, which is my name? For by this name shall ye be called at the last day;

6 And whoso taketh upon him my name, and endureth to the end, the same shall be saved at the last day.

7 Therefore, whatsoever ye shall do, ye shall do it in my name; therefore ye shall call the church in my name; and ye shall call upon the Father in my name that he will bless the church for my sake. (Book of Mormon)

I began to pray more to my Heavenly Father for a blessing to learn more about Him. I prayed to maintain my hope to get out of here and go home to Debbie. I would never allow anything again to come between her and me. My pain was so great that only the Lord could take it away. I prayed so much for so long that my heart hurt.

Yet I knew that this would soon pass and I would worship my God even more. All the gifts He had given me would be used in His service. I would stop writing now for my heart was full and tears were building in my eyes. I waited to hear the words, "Kinnith, you can go home." We were on lockdown all day. It was 11:40 and we had not been out of our cells. I was feeling down. Leaning on the Lord was what I was doing right now. I had fasted, pleaded and begged. There was no more I could do. Into the Lord's hands, I had turned over this matter.

We were finally off lockdown and I called Debbie. Debbie had not talked to anyone today. This was not good news with Debbie not hearing anything. But, I would not be moved. I was waiting for my Heavenly Father to release me from this jail so I could go home to Debbie. I would not give up. The bank had been paid. Debbie was having a tough time, but we had to go through this now instead of later. I could have been picked up in any state. If there was a road-block anywhere I would have been arrested there. I was going to be arrested somewhere, for I never even knew there was a warrant for my arrest. The Lord knew exactly what He was doing. Yet every day I lose more and more. I just did not know how I could continue my classes. I might lose my CPA. Debbie was doing her best, but this was too much for her right now. I prayed that the Lord bless her and give her peace. I will start fasting and praying to get out of here tomorrow and go home to Debbie. I thank Thee dear Heavenly Father in the name of Jesus Christ, Amen.

Chapter 20

The sister missionaries were to come back in a few days. I was not sure what they were going to teach. But I was going to be prepared. I studied the Bible and Book of Mormon daily. The Book of Mormon brought clarity to the Bible. The Book of Mormon explained Jesus Christ and his purpose in a plain language. The Book of Mormon testified of the Bible. What a powerful witness of Jesus Christ these two books provided to me. Without the Book of Mormon, I would have never considered believing in the Bible.

It was about 6:30 pm and I heard a knock at the door. It was the missionaries again. I was as prepared as possible. At some point I must start breaking the sister missionaries. They were doing such a great job that I was beginning to believe them. The missionaries asked us if we had any questions. I asked them, "Does your church have a prophet?"

They said, yes, and began to give me the history of the prophets of the Church of Jesus Christ of Latter Day Saints. I, then, asked them, "Do you all have Apostles?"

The missionaries stated, "Yes, we have twelve Apostles." Somehow, I figured that would be their answer. I continued asking questions and Sister Pickett gave answers to each question. Then all of sudden Sister Finch began to say things that had absolutely nothing to do with the conversation. She caught me off guard. I heard Sister Finch say, "I know that my Heavenly Father loves us." She went on, "I know that Jesus Christ is the Son of God."

I turned to look at her. I looked her directly in her eyes. I had learned to read people's eyes and body language to tell if a person was telling the truth. I watched her closely, every move. She continued, "I know that the Gospel of Jesus Christ has been restored to the earth." She continued, with tears running down her face, for what seemed like hours. I am sure it was not more than two minutes. I knew Sister Finch believed what she was saying with all of her heart.

I said to her, "I believe that you believe that what you have said is true." Silently, I wanted to study why she would have such a strong belief. This was a testimony. I had never heard anything like this before in my life. Her spirit spoke to my spirit. I said to her, "I want to understand your belief." Everything that they had taught me appeared to be true. If a person believed in Jesus Christ, I felt that they could not deny the Book of Mormon. They could not deny the Great Spirit these missionaries carried with them. They could not deny that this was the best chance that a believer in Jesus Christ ever had. Yet, I did not believe in the Bible or the Book of Mormon or Jesus Christ. I had two more questions I needed answered. Therefore, I asked the sisters, "Where is your church located?" The Sister missionaries were too well groomed to break. I decided to go after the members of the church for I knew that the members were weak. So I invited myself to their church. Here is why. I wanted to see for myself if they had paid ministry. I would never join a church where the ministry gets paid to share the gospel. I was sure that their minister made a living selling the Gospel of Jesus Christ.

When Jesus was on the earth, He never charged people to hear Him preach. He never charged for healings. He gave the gospel freely.

Jesus called his Disciples and taught them to give the gospel freely to anyone who would listen. Every Christian preacher that I have ever met was in the business of selling the gospel. They preached the gospel for money. I am sure that most of them did not start out that way. However, in the past twenty years more people have left a church to start their own church for the pure love of money. They may say good things yet they would always end up taking money for their services. Preaching is a great business today. I could never join a church where I have to pay a preacher a salary for him to preach the gospel that God gave him/her freely. I have always said, "If God called you to preach, when he calls me to pay you then I will." Check the scriptures yourself. Learn what the Bible says about those who sell the Gospel. So I wanted to attend the sister's church to see the collection plate go around. I wanted to see the preacher get up and put on a show. I had seen this so many times. I would not even go to church to see these acts. The better the show, the more people follow, the more money the preacher makes.

I told the Sister missionaries that I would show up at their church at 10:00 because I had some things already scheduled. Debbie and I showed up at the church at 10:00. You would not believe how the members welcomed us. Yet we were used to this type of welcome, for most people are this way in the South. The members took us to the missionaries. Sister Pickett and Sister Finch were so excited to see us. What we did not know is that most people who tell the missionaries that they are coming to church never show up. I do not remember much about this visit. I do know that there was not a collection plate passed. I thought the collection must have occurred in the first hour. Maybe the full church did not make the collection because they knew I was coming to church. I told Debbie, "Let's not tell them when we are coming back to visit their church." This way they could not get together and plan how to deceive us. We decided to come back to the church without letting the missionaries know of the date.

We showed up at church unannounced the next time. The missionaries were glad to see us. They had me sit next to a man named Gus Sanback. My family was at church early this time. Being early did not allow the church members to plan for our attendance. I waited for the collection to take place. I knew they did not have time to stop the collection because they did not know I would be there. There was not a collection! I was shocked. Not only was there no collection, but people from the congregation did all of the preaching. This was a strange concept, yet I was impressed. I asked Gus, "Did you know there are books missing from the Bible?"

Gus stated, "Yes, and I will get you a list of them."

Shocking! Who could possibly know this? I was truly shocked. These people, at this church, had great knowledge of the Bible. I went home that day feeling that this could be the true church of Jesus Christ. However, this was not possible; there couldn't be a true Christian Church or a church with the true gospel. I began to study even more. I had to break this church somehow. I looked at Joseph Smith. He had a lot of baggage. Yet he met all the qualifications of the prophets of old. I attacked the Book of Mormon. I could not break the Book of Mormon. I attacked the Bible. The Bible was weak. I could break it, yet the Book of Mormon closed all the holes in the Bible. The other scriptures this church had could not be broken. These scriptures were too well-written, it had to be from God. Now, I had only one question left. "What was I going to do if they could answer this question?" I was sure the missionaries could not answer this question! There had not been a church that had ever answered the first question. Now here was a church that had answered five of the six questions. "When do I ask them the sixth question?" I would ask the final question at our next meeting. I wondered what I would I do if they could answer the last question. I wasn't worried because I was sure the Sister missionaries couldn't answer this question.

Chapter 21

Day 15

It had been another long night but I was at peace. I think by now anyone reading this book knows the routine. However, I will go through it again so that you will understand the situation. I got very little sleep. I had been fasting and praying all night. It was morning. Today was the same as yesterday: wake up at 5:00 am, get out of bed and stand at the door of the cell. The guard began his count due to a guard shift change. After the count, I lay back in the bed for about an hour. It was time for breakfast. I finished eating breakfast and began cleaning my cell. Cleaning the cell included cleaning the toilet, washing down the metal mirror, making the bed and sweeping the floor. I thought, man, how do these people put up with this for so long? I had seen people get out of jail and then come back three to five days later. This might sound familiar.

I decided to adjust my mind and heart for the long haul. I could actually be here for another three weeks. That is a long time and each day I lose more financially. I was thinking it was not that long ago when Debbie and I had retired from jobs. We had built enough money that we did not have to work. However, after losing hundreds of thousands of dollars in our nine-year stay in Louisiana we finally left Louisiana and moved to Utah. We made it to Utah with nothing left. We even had to borrow money on the way to Utah. Our debt load was massive and the future was not looking good at all. Over the last year, we had made great progress financially but there were great sums of money we owed. Now all of that progress had gone down the drain. Every day that I was in jail, the more financial progress was lost. I had created plans on how to start over based on the estimated day I hoped to get out of this place. The worst case was that I would be locked up for three more weeks. If the city of Baton Rouge did not pick me up, Utah County Jail would have to release me. I just prayed that I did not have to go to Louisiana by prisoner bus. The story was that it could take up to two months to get to Baton Rouge because the bus stops in multiple cities on the way to pickup other prisoners to be dropped off in difference cities along the way. I could end up staying in multiple jails along the way. I prayed that this would not happen to me. I talked to one guy who claimed it took three weeks to be transferred from Oregon to California due to all the stops. Many bad things could happen in this scenario. I would never share this information with Debbie because I thought it would be too much for her. I was thinking that this was too much for me too. Well, these matters were in the Lord's hands. All I could do was brace myself for whatever came next.

We were still in lockup. We were waiting for our break. The guys from the bottom cells were out in the bay area. We have a big spades tournament scheduled for the day. My partner and I had not lost a game yet. This time we were playing against a guy who was very good. We were the best spade players here, mainly because we were the only ones who had played the game before. Interesting that in the South spades was a big deal. In the West, only a few people had ever heard of the game. Well it was time to get out of here. I would call Debbie first and hope there was some good news. I thought, man, I sure could use something positive today. I spoke with Debbie. Now, three lawyers and one judge had confirmed, "There is no amount of money that can get me out of jail." The only way I could get out of jail was for the city of Baton Rouge to send someone to Utah to escort me back to Louisiana. Or, I stayed in this jail for three more weeks. Based on everything I had heard to this point, it appeared that my case was not important enough for Baton Rouge to spend money to bring me there. It appeared I would be here for a while. I really did not want Debbie to know this.

I got off the phone and back into the spades game. The guy I mentioned earlier was very good at this game. Therefore, it would come down to which partner played the best. On this day, my partner turned out to be the one. With his efforts, we were able to win the tournament. Therefore, for lunch today we would get to take whatever we want from the losers' plates. It was truly a sad day, yet I was trying to make the best of it.

Just think to yourself for one moment. You awake early in the morning. You take a shower and assist your wife in cooking breakfast. You and your wife eat breakfast and begin planning your day. You discuss things you want to accomplish this day. You make plans to get back together later in the day. You discuss dinner and where and what you will eat. You start making plans as to what you are going to do for the rest of the week. Everything is going your way. Life has been good to you. You and your wife go downstairs to prepare the car and confirm you have the gas you need. You say a prayer for your family and all of your friends. You thank the Lord for all the blessings in your life. You pray for all missionaries around the world. You say a special prayer for that missionary who is your son. You open the garage and back out to head on your way for the day. You pull out of your condominium complex and turn on to the main road. And then everything changes, and you unexpectedly find yourself locked up in jail and have no idea when you will be released. You have to spend over a thousand dollars just to get some idea of why you are in jail. Fifteen days later, three lawyers, a judge and your wife cannot get you out of jail. Now that is a nightmare for you. However, I tell you this is not a nightmare, this was real and I was living it in that jail.

Still as bad as this was, it could have been worse. I met some guys in jail who would be moved to federal prison for twenty and thirty years. What kind of life would that be? I went to court with a guy a few weeks ago that was here because of selling drugs. He had served about four months in jail. He was scheduled to be released from jail eight days ago. On his way to court, he was able to read a newspaper the guard had. He read about a three-year-old girl that had overdosed on drugs. The little girl was in the hospital and they were not sure she was going to make it. The mother was arrested, and put in jail for drug use and abuse of a minor. This was pretty bad. However, it got worse. He realized that this was his wife and daughter! He had gotten himself straight and now this. He found out later in court that his daughter had made it. Since no one could find the father of the child, the state had taken her. Now he found himself standing in court, ready to be released, so he could go home to take care of his daughter. As he stood before the judge with much sadness, but great hope, the judge told him, "You will not be released today." The guy broke down into tears. He told the judge about his daughter. The judge knew of the story, but could not release him. I watched this man cry like a baby, not for himself but for his daughter. The deal was he was getting out early for good behavior but one of his guards did not sign the proper document. The judge's hands were tied and there was not anything the judge could do. No one could find the guard to sign the paperwork. So the guy had to stay in jail. His next court date was today. He was leaving later to go home. He was the person on the team I just played in spades. He was the other good player. I prayed for him and his daughter many nights. On this day, he and his daughter would be together!

Dinner was okay and I waited to call Debbie. Steve and I discussed the gospel again. He was making progress. His main hangup in trusting the gospel was that the people who killed his people and stole his country brought the gospel to him. I began to give him a history of Blacks in America. He realized that the Blacks place in

America had not been a good one. He had heard stories about the conditions of my people throughout our history in America. He then asked me, "How can you join the Mormon Church when there are so many black churches you could have joined?"

I told him that there were no true Black churches. He said that he had seen many Black churches and had attended some. I asked him, "When Blacks came to America how many Black churches existed in America?" He said he did not think any existed. I told him that he was right. I then asked him, "Did Christian slave owners allow the salves to join their churches?" He said I would think that no slave owners allowed salves to join their churches. Again, I said you are right. Then I asked him, "What denomination do you think the slave owners where, who denied the salves from entering their church-es?" He said he did not know. I told him almost no Christian church would allow Blacks to attend their church, except one. He asked me, "Which church would allow Blacks to attend?" I told him the Church of Jesus Christ of Latter Day Saints. The people you call Mormons. He said really. I told him that if there was a Black church, it would be the Church of Jesus Christ of Latter Day Saints. I suggested that if he checked history he would discover that most Christian denominations did not allow a black man to enter their churches. Instead, the slave owner would tell the slaves that there was a place made for them. You are a Baptist because I own you and tell you what you are. The slave owner is the true Baptist. Since he will not allow the slave to worship the true Baptist religion, then what religion is the slave worshipping? This is why even today, when you go into a town there are two first Baptist churches. One is white and one is black. Steve understood and his concept of black and white churches began to change.

It was time to call Debbie. I was so happy that AJ was on his mis-sion and didn't know anything of this matter. Kenneth was adjusting to military life. He was too busy to wonder why he had not heard from me. Tiffany had her hands full with life. I wondered if she had noticed that I hadn't called her for her birthday. Debbie did not have any more news. She was holding up the best she could. Our church family was there for her should she need anything. I really did not want my siblings to know about this. My siblings would break down the gates of hell to get me out of this issue. This was why I wouldn't burden them with this matter. I was going to bed now. I was ready for the long haul. I would not waiver or give in to my situation. I would stay focused and prepare for recovering after getting out of here.

Chapter 22

There was a knock at the door, it was the missionaries. This was the night that I would ask them question number six. The missionaries spoke concerning a few things. Finally, the missionaries asked, "Do you believe the Book of Mormon is true?"

Debbie spoke up and stated, "I believe the Book of Mormon is true."

When I heard this I said, "Debbie you cannot say that." I remembered when the missionaries first came to my home, and they had asked, "If you find the things we share with you to be true, would you be baptized?" We said yes. Now Debbie has just stated, "She knew the Book of Mormon was true." Now I felt she would have to be baptized. So I said, "Debbie, you cannot say that!" Yet she had said it and could not take it back. I told the missionaries, "I am not sure that I believed the Book of Mormon is true."

It was time for me to ask question six to save Debbie. I asked the missionaries, "What is God's plan for those people who have never heard of the Gospel, but lived a good life and died?"

The missionaries stopped me. They stated, "We will answer that question on our next visit." I was disappointed. I felt that they hadn't answered the question because they did not have an answer. I wasn't really disappointed, I was glad they did not have an answer. I had finally found a crack in this church. The Sister missionaries left and we set up another appointment.

I used the four days to set up my question. I needed to back up my question with logic and the scriptures. I had used this question twenty years earlier at the University of Southern Mississippi before a religious panel. Now I would use it again to break the Church of Jesus Christ of Latter Day Saints. By the way, these people called themselves Mormons, but they were the truest Christians I had ever met.

The day came. There was a knock at the door and Debbie invited the missionaries into our home. The missionaries wanted to talk about different subjects, but I did not want to hear anything from them. I had a question and I needed to hear their answer. I interrupted the Sister missionaries discussion and began to set up my main question. The flow of the conversation went as follows:

I asked the Sister missionaries, "Is God a good God?"

The missionaries stated, "Yes, God is a good God."

I stated to the missionaries, "You told me that God is our Heavenly Father?"

The missionaries stated, "Yes, He is our Heavenly Father."

I asked, "Is Jesus the Son of the God?"

The missionaries stated, "Yes, Jesus is the Son of God."

I asked, "So whatever Jesus says is true?"

The missionaries stated, "Yes whatever Jesus says is true."

I asked the Sisters, "Would you say that this scripture is true?"

John 3:1-10 (KJV)
"1 There was a man of the Pharisees, named Nicodemus, a ruler of the Jews:
2 The same came to Jesus by night, and said unto him, Rabbi, we know that thou art a teacher come from God: for no man can do these miracles that thou doest, except God be with him.
3 Jesus answered and said unto him, Verily, verily, I say unto thee, Except a man be born again, he cannot see the kingdom of God.
4 Nicodemus saith unto him, How can a man be born when he is old? can he enter the second time into his mother's womb, and be born?
5 Jesus answered, Verily, verily, I say unto thee, Except a man be born of water and of the Spirit, he cannot enter into the kingdom of God.
6 That which is born of the flesh is flesh; and that which is born of the Spirit is spirit.
7 Marvel not that I said unto thee, Ye must be born again.
8 The wind bloweth where it listeth, and thou hearest the sound thereof, but canst not tell whence it cometh, and whither it goeth: so is every one that is born of the Spirit.
9 Nicodemus answered and said unto him, How can these things be?
10 Jesus answered and said unto him, Art thou a master of Israel, and knowest not these things?"

The missionaries stated, "These scriptures are true."

I asked, "In Verse 5, does born of water means being baptized?"

The missionaries stated, "Yes, it means being baptized."

I asked, "Would you say that this scripture is true?"

> 1st Peter 3:18-19
> **"18** For Christ also hath once suffered for sins, the just for the unjust,that he might bring us to God, being put to death in the flesh, but quickened by the Spirit:
> **19** By which also he went and preached unto the spirits in prison;
> **20** Which sometime were disobedient, when once the long-suffering of God waited in the days of Noah, while the ark was a preparing, wherein few, that is, eight souls were saved by water.
> **21** The like figure whereunto even baptism doth also now save us (not the putting away of the filth of the flesh, but the answer of a good conscience toward God, by the resurrection of Jesus Christ:"

The missionaries stated, "These scriptures are true."

The stage was set. I got the missionaries to commit to all of the questions and scriptures just as we did the religious leaders twenty years ago in college. Now I could ask the question that I asked those ministers twenty years ago.

> I stated, "There were millions of people who lived on the earth before Jesus was born. Millions of these people lived great lives, yet they were never baptized because they knew not Jesus Christ. There are millions of people who lived at the time that Jesus was on earth and never heard of Him. Millions of them lived great lives. Yet they were never baptized. Since Jesus has died until today, there are millions of people who have never heard of Jesus Christ. Million of these people lived great lives and were never baptized."

The missionaries agreed with these statements.

Then I asked, "Then tell me, what will happen to these people on judgment day?" I was sure that the missionaries would not have a good answer to this question. You see, if their answer was anything other than these people who were never baptized could not enter the Kingdom of God, then they would contradict these scriptures:

> **3** Jesus answered and said unto him, Verily, verily, I say unto thee, Except a man be born again, he cannot see the kingdom of God.
> **4** Nicodemus saith unto him, How can a man be born when he is old? can he enter the second time into his mother's womb, and be born?
> **5** Jesus answered, Verily, verily, I say unto thee, Except a man be born of water and of the Spirit, he cannot enter into the kingdom of God.

Now if by some chance the missionaries had some weird answer, I added this question, "For what reason did Jesus go into the spirit world to preach to spirits? The spirits could not be baptized since they do not have a body. Therefore, Jesus would be condemning these spirits. This would mean that God is not a good God."

I had made my stand and wanted to hear what the missionaries had to say.

These missionaries quickly asked me, "What do you think Jesus taught the spirits in the spirits world?"

I said, "For Jesus to be fair, He could only teach them: faith, belief in Christ and baptism. He would only teach the same things he taught on earth."

The missionaries stated that I was correct. Then the missionaries shocked me by explaining a concept that answered both of my questions. This concept was baptism for the dead. The ideal is a person who is alive can be baptized for someone who is dead. Now this concept satisfies, "What happens to people who never heard of Jesus Christ and died?" The concept satisfies the reason Jesus went to the Spirit World to teach the spirits. I asked the missionaries, "Where are these baptisms for the dead done?"

The missionaries stated, "In the Temple."

I immediately remembered that the "molten sea" mentioned in 1ˢᵗ Kings 7:23-25 (KJV) was located in the temple Solomon built. Could this be a baptism font?

23 ¶ And he made a molten sea, ten cubits from the one brim to the other: it was round all about, and his height was five cubits: and a line of thirty cubits did compass it round about. **24** And under the brim of it round about there were knops compassing it, ten in a cubit, compassing the sea round about: the knops were cast in two rows, when it was cast. **25** It stood upon twelve oxen, three looking toward the north, and three looking toward the west, and three looking toward the south, and three looking toward the east: and the sea was set above upon them, and all their hinder parts were inward.

I remembered Paul speaking of this concept in 1 Corinthians 15:29:

"29 Else what shall they do which are baptized for the dead, if the dead rise not at all? why are they then baptized for the dead?"

Where did these missionaries get this concept? How do they know this? Has the Gospel been restored? How can I deny what I have heard and studied? The Sister missionaries answered all six of my questions? Where do I go from here? The missionaries left that night around 8:30 pm. I was in shock from this new information. These missionaries had answered all of my questions.

I did not sleep much for the next couple of days. How could it be possible that Christianity was true? How could it be possible that the Church of Jesus Christ of Latter Day Saints had the fullness of the Gospel? My God, was this true? Had I found the power that runs the universe? Could this power that runs the universe actually be Jesus Christ via our Heavenly Father?

Chapter 23

Day 16

I heard the guard call my name! I awoke and glanced at the clock on the wall through the glass peep window to my cell. I saw from the clock that it was 4:00 am. Was I dreaming? No, I was not dreaming. I really heard my name! The guard was calling me stating these words, "Kinnith Holloway, get packed, you have a flight to Baton Rouge, Louisiana!" I thought, "The time is here!" You see, I knew that I would have to go to Baton Rouge. There in Baton Rouge was my only way out of this trouble. It was really bad that I did not even know the full story as to why I was locked up until I got to Baton Rouge. Well, here I was going to the one place I did not want to go, yet I had to go.

I pulled the mattress and sheets from my bed. I picked up all of my belongings, said goodbye to my cellmate and headed down stairs to meet the guard. I told my cellmate that I would contact him on the outside when I got back to Utah. Once I was downstairs, I met the guard. The guard told me to go out the door, take a right and go down the hallway. He told me that someone would meet me at the end of the hallway. I asked the guard, "Is there any way I can call my wife to let her know that I was being transferred to Louisiana?"

The guard said, "No, no one can know that you are being transferred."

I went down the hallway, knowing that Debbie had no idea that I was leaving Utah. This was very painful because Debbie would be all alone in Utah and not even know it. I reached the end of the hallway. The guard was there and told me to go meet another guard. I walked about twenty yards to another guard that took my bed pad and sheets. She then told me to go down another hallway. At the end of this hallway was the front desk to the jail facility. The guard at the front desk told me a sheriff officer from Baton Rouge, LA was coming to pick me up. The sheriff officers were running late so I was locked in a small cell to wait for them. The cell they put me in was about 4ft by 4ft with a commode and a bench. It was so cold in this cell that I could not go to sleep. I stayed in this cell for what seemed like an hour. Just as I was about to dose off, the cell door opened. There standing in front of me were the sheriff officers, one male and one female. The desk guard came over and brought me a bag that contained my clothes that I wore when I was first arrested. The desk guard stated, "You need to check that everything you had when you came to the jail is in the bag." Everything was in the bag except my wallet. I told the desk guard that my wallet was missing. The desk guard stated, "Your wife took your wallet when she came to pick up the auto insurance papers." I remembered that Debbie had to come to the jail on the second day to pick up those papers. Debbie was not supposed to pick up my wallet, yet they gave it to her. Then the male sheriff officer asked the female officer to leave the room. The officer told me to take off all of my clothes. He searched me to confirm that I did not have anything on me. Then he told me to put on the clothes that the desk guard had given me (my clothes). I put on my clothes. I told the officer that I was glad to see him. The officer seemed very concerned that I was glad to see him. The officer told me a few things that I will not write. I said to him very politely, "Yes, I understand." Then the female officer came into the cell. I told her that I was glad to see her also. She seemed puzzled. Then she asked, "Why would you be glad to see me?"

I told her "I have lost my job, maybe my business and maybe my house. The only way I could get out of this trouble was to go to Baton Rouge. If you all would not have come I was to stay in jail for another three weeks!"

She said to me, "Going to Baton Rouge is not necessarily a good thing."

I told her, "I know but it is my only way out." Now the male officer had been listening.

He asked me, "What did you do? You just don't seem like someone who should be in jail." I said, "I agree with you, yet here I am and I need to see my way out of this trouble. You guys are my next step."

The two officers talked to each other for about a minute. The male officer said, "I have to put hand cuffs on you. I am supposed to put cuffs on your ankles and run a chain from your ankle to the cuffs on your wrist." Then he said, "I am not going to do that to you. I will put this brace on your right leg. We have a tracking system for this brace so do not try anything." He also stated that he would shoot me should I try to get away at the airport. I told him that I would not consider attempting a getaway. So he put the brace on my leg. The brace weighed about twenty pounds.

Finally, I was leaving the jail complex after fifteen days. We went outside to get into the sheriff officers' car. The two sheriff officers got into the front and I got into the back seat. We drove out of the compound headed to the airport. This was about a forty-five mile drive. Sitting in the back seat of the car, I knew I was headed to a very bad place in Baton Rouge. You see, the city of Baton Rouge loves to put people in their federal prison instead of the city jail. The federal prison is not a good place to be. As the car went down the highway toward the airport, we passed the exit where I live. I felt the pain of Debbie not knowing that I was leaving Utah. I could feel her spirit touch my spirit as I passed by that exit. I said a prayer for her. We passed the temple that I attended. I looked at the temple and said, "I will return." We continued down the highway and I passed two more temples. The temples were beautiful and I knew that the Lord was with me. As we drew near the airport, I prayed to the Lord to harden my heart and prepare me for whatever was next. It had been fifteen days since I was home or had seen Debbie. The last temple I passed was the Salt Lake Temple. I knew the airport was about ten minutes away. I braced myself and turned inward to protect myself.

We were at the airport and the officer placed a jacket over my hands to attempt to hide the handcuffs before we entered the terminal. It is a terrible feeling walking into the airport with handcuffs on. All of the people know that you are some type of criminal when you have on handcuffs. It also did not help that of the two thousand people in the airport; there may have been fifty blacks. I was one of the fifty and I was in handcuffs! I surely represented my people well this day. We picked up our boarding passes and headed to the gate. I did not know this. But, there is a special area of the airport that allows the sheriff to bring his gun onto the plane. This was the area where we checked in. It was about 7:30 am and I had not eaten anything this morning.

While I was sitting at the gate waiting for the plane, about fifteen missionaries came and sat in the area near me. I overheard them talking about going to Richmond, Virginia on their mission. I wanted to speak with the missionaries because they were going to the same mission that AJ was serving. However, I had on handcuffs! I could not speak to the missionaries for I could see them saying, "AJ we met your dad and he was in handcuffs!" This was not a good feeling.

Therefore, I did not say anything. The wait for the flight was about an hour. Finally, we were starting to board the flight. A number of people were able to see that I was handcuffed but they never said a word. The male sheriff and I sat in the last two back seats on the plane. I really dislike riding at the back of the plane but here I was. The flight took off and I tried to sleep as much as possible. I was very hungry and thirsty. When the flight attendant came by to offer drinks, I took one. It is not easy trying to drink a soda with handcuffs on. I was able to complete the task but not without some tough times. I also had to make sure I did not need to use the bathroom on the plane. This would have been an even tougher task.

The plane finally landed in Houston. Now I had to go out and face all these people. People gave me this strange look when they saw the handcuffs. The flight to Houston was late and we had to go across the airport terminal to reach the connecting flight. I had to walk very fast and the deputy could not allow me out of his sight. This was a very tough walk. It was around noon and I was becoming very weak from all this physical movement without food or water. I kept thinking how my ancestors worked all day without water and were beaten at the same time and they made it. I was sure I would make it also. Finally, we were at the terminal. I was very tired and hungry. We boarded the plane and were on our way to Baton Rouge. I continued to pray to the Lord to strengthen me for I knew what awaited me in a state prison. In Baton Rouge, they housed almost everyone in the state prison. This is not a good place for anyone to be and that was where I was headed. I was getting off the plane to enter the Baton Rouge airport terminal. The sheriff told me to go out the luggage door instead of going into the terminal. I went out the luggage door and down the ramp. There was a police car waiting for me on the tarmac. They put me into the police car and told me I was going to the Baton Rouge Federal Prison. This was not a surprise to me for I knew that this was going to be the case once I got to Baton Rouge. The sheriff deputy told the police officer that I was the easiest person he had ever picked up. I was silent. I did not have anything to say. I knew I was going to maybe the worst place I had ever been, but I was ready. This was my only way out.

We drove to a very large fence, it opened, and we went through. Then a second fence opened and we drove through that one also. We pulled up to a black door. The car stopped and we got out of the car. The deputy told me to follow him. I did. The black door opened and we went in. When the black door closed behind me, I knew there was no way for me to get out. I had just left a jail compound that was 95% white to enter a prison that was 98% black. I had just left a jail compound that treated you like a human to enter a place that treated you like a wild animal. I must admit that 90% of the people I met since I entered the prison acted like wild animals. I was standing waiting to be processed into the prison. I heard so many curse words and so much vulgar language that it made me sick. Not physically, but spiritually sick. The guards at the prison were the only ones who seemed to be sane. However, the guards had to be mean or the prisoners would run over them. The bad thing was that I was only at the front door of the prison! I asked the Lord to let me remember all the bad things that I went through in the some of the foreign countries I had been. I had to get my mind right to deal with this environment for it was like going into a jungle of wild animals. I thought to myself that these were my people, but over 80% of them appeared to have no regard for life.

They fingerprinted me and took my picture. The chief guard asked me what I was doing there. He told me you do not belong here. I told him my situation. I told him, "I have not even seen the information that I am charged with."

He told me to wait and he would get me the details. He came back with the information and for the first time in 15 days, I saw why I was in prison. He said this is not worth you being in prison. All you need to do is pay this debt off and you are out of here. He said he could not believe that I was arrested and brought all the way from Utah for this. He told me if we had time, we would let you out today but a judge would have to do it. He told me the only reason you are here is that you missed your court date. He asked me why I did not show up for court (over 14 months ago). I told the chief guard that I moved from Baton Rouge over thirteen months ago and never received a summons. He said but someone had to sign the summons. I told him that I had no idea who could have signed it but it was not me. He then told me I would need about $700 and I would be out tomorrow once I spoke to a judge. I thanked this man and went to the next location. Here was an example of the Lord placing the right people in your path as you move forward. There was no such thing as speaking something into existence without work. You must move first and then the Lord will assist you when you cannot see your way to continue.

This area, where I was located, was called intake. This was where they processed you into the prison. In this area, there were four male and two female holding cells. Each male cell could hold about 20 people. There were about 40 men in each of the first three cells and about five men in the other cell. There were about ten women in one of their cells and the other cell for women was empty. When I checked in through intake, I did not say a word. I was wearing a BYU shirt that totally did not fit in LSU country. Immediately, the guys got on my case. There were some very evil words used, but I ignored them. I wanted to avoid all confrontations in this environment. If I had said anything confrontational, then I would have to defend myself. I was locked in the holding cell with five other guys. By this time, it was around 4:00 pm and I had not eaten anything. I was very hungry, tired and sleepy. All of us in the cell began to feel each other out. These were some pretty decent guys in this cell and we all got along well. There were benches along the side of the walls and on the back wall was a toilet. There was a four-foot wall, which came out about six feet out from the wall to hide the toilet. The guys in the other cells were cursing and starting fights. It was a horrible situation. I maintained my cool and avoided getting involved. There were two females that came into the intake area and the guys went wild. They acted as if they had never seen a woman before. The guys said some unbelievable sexual things to these women. I really felt bad for those women. Then I heard these women use some vulgar language. I will not write these words for the words have no value. I did not feel sorry for them any longer. These women could handle themselves very well.

An hour passed and finally they brought us food. The cursing and vulgar speaking had not slowed at all. There were about thirty of us in this cell. There was nowhere to sit and standing room was tight. The food was given out through a small opening in the cell door. A third of us were sitting on the benches. Another third were standing. The others were sitting on the floor. I think that animals are treated better than this! The food was good. I had not had very much spicy food in Utah. Interesting, I do not eat dark meat chicken, but this day I ate dark meat chicken. After eating, I felt much better but I found myself in a place that no one would want to be. As it got later, more inmates were brought in. About twenty of us were moved from my current cell to one of the other cells that were already overloaded. Now, I was in a cell with about seventy people. There was not room to sit on a bench or on the floor. We were just standing and this was where I would spend the night.

It was very cold. There were many requests for mattress pads or blankets but there were none given. This was one of the most horrible nights of my life. Just trying to find some way to sleep was nearly impossible. I would sleep ten minutes lying on a hard floor. Then change places with someone to sleep sitting on the hard bench or learn to sleep standing up. This was where I was and I would not wish this upon my worst enemy. All night, more people kept coming into the prison. There was no room but they keep coming. The police brought women and men into the prison all night. Cursing, vulgar language and fighting continued throughout the night. All types of odors filled the cell. This environment would drive a sane person crazy, yet over half of the people here had been here before. However, I had one thing in my favor; the Lord allowed me the ability to harden my heart and mind. The Lord strengthened me and I knew I would get through this. My greatest worry was that Debbie did not know where I was. She probably thought I was still in Utah and just did not call her today. The authorities would not allow me to call Debbie to let her know where I was. I prayed to my Heavenly Father to take care of her. I prayed to my Heavenly Father to take care of AJ while he was serving his mission. I prayed to my Heavenly Father to take care of Tiffany and Kenneth. I learned to pray for others even in my time of need. I cannot end this chapter with "good night" for there was no sleep for me.

Chapter 24

I **was preparing** for a trip to St. George, UT. I wanted to go see the temple that was located there. I had begun to believe that the people I was in business with in Utah were members of the Church of Jesus Christ of Latter Day Saints. I was going to ask them when I got to St. George. On the flight over, I contemplated all the things I had heard and studied. The Sister missionaries had brought so much information into my life. My heart was very heavy for there was no way to deny the truth. Yet how could this be true! What these missionaries had shared with me would make Christianity true. This would mean that Jesus Christ and His Heavenly Father was the source of the power that ran the universe!

Upon arriving in St. George, I went to my friend and business partner's home to ask him if he was a member of the Church of Jesus Christ of Latter Day Saints. When I entered his home, hanging over the fireplace, I saw a picture of Jesus Christ. I knew the Church of Jesus Christ of Latter Day Saints was the only church that used that picture. I did not have to ask my friend if he was a member of the Church of Jesus Christ of Latter Day Saints, I knew it.

I spent the next day in business meetings. When we got a break from the meeting, Debbie and I went to the temple in St. George. I was glad to hear that a person had to earn the right to go into the temple. In days of old, people had to earn the right to go into the temple also. Anyone could go onto the temple grounds. While we were at the St. George Temple, we visited the temple visitor's center. There were many great things to see and read while we were there. When we entered the visitor's center, there was a woman sitting at a desk. Debbie and I were in the center. Then, from somewhere a man showed up. I don't know where he came from, yet he came over to talk with me. Debbie and I were looking at pictures of the many different temples around the world. This guy showed me a picture of the Atlanta Temple. I knew this building. I lived in Atlanta for nine years. Every day, on my way to work, I would pass this building. Then Debbie walked off to review other things. I tried to leave also but this guy would not separate himself from me. He began to tell me many things about the Bible's history and the gospel. Just to let him know he was not speaking to a rookie, I mentioned Moses marrying an Ethiopian woman. The man told me many stories concerning this matter. He told me many things about the African people and their religions. There were so many things he told me, that I could not even write all of them. Now I became very interested in this man. I begin to ask him many questions. He answered every question I asked. Then a strange thing happened. I was about to ask him a question and he answered the question before I could ask. He did this about four or five times. Every question that came to my mind, he would answer it before I asked the question. I began to realize the man was reading my mind! Just to be sure, I thought of another question and the guy answered the question before I ask. This confirmed that this man was reading my mind! I went and told Debbie. "Debbie, you would not believe this, but that guy (pointing to him) will answer any question I think of before I ask the question." I told Debbie a question that I was thinking of and asked her to go with me to talk to this man. When Debbie and I reached the man, he answered the question before I asked. Now I knew it was true. Debbie and I tested it again and the man answered the question before I asked. I knew then that this was not an ordinary man. Debbie left to go to another area of the room while I studied this man. I questioned the man for about 20 minutes. He seemed to have unlimited knowledge concerning the history of the world especially religion. There were some things I saw concerning this man that I will not write. I have told the story of the things that I will not write today. However, it suffices to use a scripture that will give you an idea of what I saw. I will use the words of the Apostle Paul:

2nd Corinthians 12:2-3
2 I knew a man in Christ above fourteen years ago, (whether in the body, I cannot tell; or whether out of the body, I cannot tell: God knoweth;) such a one caught up to the third heaven.
3 And I knew such a man, (whether in the body, or out of the body, I cannot tell: God knoweth;)

The man I met and talked to this day was not of this world! He wanted to tell me many other things, but we needed to get back to the business meeting. As we walked out of the visitor center, a thought came to my mind. This was the thought, "The man you spoke with was never in the building." I grabbed Debbie's hand and told her the thought, which was spoken to my mind. I told Debbie that we should go back into the visitor's center, because the man was never there. I turned to look through the glass doors of the visitor's center and saw no one but the woman sitting at the desk. Yet Debbie was afraid to go back into the center and we left. This was a major turning point in my thinking.

Once our business meetings were completed, we drove to Las Vegas to catch a flight home. On our flight home from St. George, I began reading one of the books I brought from the visitor center. The book was about the three Nephrites (Book of Mormon) who never died. These Book of Mormon prophets never died for they requested of Jesus to live until the second coming. Could I have seen one of them? I do not know who it was I saw and talked with but there was one thing I knew I had to do. I had to join the Church of Jesus Christ of Latter Day Saints. This would be the first church I had ever joined.

Neither my Mother nor Father was alive now to see this happen. They both passed away about a year before this date. This was a decision I would have to make on my own. I began to review all of my thoughts concerning the Bible, the Quran and the Book of Mormon. I thought of all the years I studied world religions and every denomination of Christianity. I thought about all the churches and ministers I had attended and met. I thought of my Mother, Father, and all of my brothers and sisters. I considered my wife and children. I concluded that I had found the power that controls the universe. Now I would have to do something about it. We returned from Utah and I still had so many things on my mind.

Chapter 25

Day 17

I **was half-awake;** half-asleep, I was not sure which. I was not sure what time it was. In fact, I was not sure of much of anything right then. I heard the guard shouting for us to wake up. There must have been at least seventy-five of us in a cell whose capacity was forty. There were people everywhere! The guards told us to stand and create lines. There were about twelve lines and about eight people in each line. There were many others in the other cells. There was a lot of cursing and vulgar language coming from all directions. No one had taken a shower and the odor almost made me want to throw up. Breakfast passed through the cell bars and the first in line passed breakfast back until everyone had breakfast. We had to eat standing and the food was terrible or might have been good, I couldn't tell. This was just a horrible time in my life. Breakfast was finally over and the guards were checking to make sure no one kept any items. In here, everything was a weapon or some way to make a drug. For this reason, the guards wanted every cup, piece of paper or anything that could be used to create any type of weapon. This was not a place that anyone should be.

The guard announced that they would be calling the name of all people who would be attending court today. Lord knows I needed to be one of those who would attend court. For attending court was the only way out of this prison. I prayed that they call my name. The guard began calling the names of those who would attend court. After the guard called about thirty names, I heard the best sound I had heard in years. "Kinnith Holloway, you will attend court today." I was so excited to attend court. I really needed to get out of this prison. This was a very dangerous place. Everyone who was attending court was wishing the others good luck. After all of the guys had acted so inhuman for the last 24 hours, I found out that these guys were sane after all. In prison, about sixty percent of the inmates are cool. The other forty percent are really crazy! But everyone has to act a certain way to survive. Survival is what it is all about when you are in a place like this. I have been in some tough places before but in all cases there was a way out that I controlled. But in this place, there was no way out that was in my control.

The time was here. Of the over three hundred inmates in holding cells, about eighty of us went into a room that seated about one hundred people. We lined up in rows of about ten to leave our holding cell. The guards checked everyone for weapons and drugs. Oh yes, there were weapons and drugs even in the holding cells. You would be surprised at how these guys could get things that should not be in prison. As I entered the room, I saw a large monitor on the wall. I was not sure what the room was for, but I was under the impression that we would be handcuffed and taken to the courthouse. Instead, this monitor was there to display the courthouse and we would meet the judge via this monitor. I was able to sit in row fourteen. I was trying to sit with guys who did not fit in prison. After we all were seated, the guards turned the monitor on and nothing happened. The monitor was not working! How could this be possible for I knew if this monitor did not work, I would not see the judge today? This would be another long day in prison. I knew I would not stay in the holding cell for another day. I would be processed into the real prison and I wanted no part of that. The guards worked on the monitor trying to get it to work with no luck. I wanted to ask the guards to allow me to fix it. I had the skills to get this thing working and I was more than willing to give my service. Then the monitor came on after about twenty minutes. I could see the courtroom via the monitor. I was so happy because now I had a chance to get out of this horrible place. Finally, after about ten more minutes court was in session and someone in the courtroom stated, "All arise for the honorable Judge Sherry." She was an attractive woman of about fifty years. She said hello to all of us and gave us an overview of what would happen from this point. She told us that she was not there to decide if we are guilty or innocent, but to decide how much our bail would be so that we could be released today. She made it clear that we would have to pay the bail or stay in prison until the bail is paid or until our court date.

These were the greatest words I had heard in a long time. I knew I was getting out of lockup today! The Lord had heard my prayer and had shown me favor. Then she asked for the first inmate.

The doors open and a guy came in chained up. He had a chain around his neck that ran to his waist, then down his legs to cuffs on his ankles. He did not have a shirt on and he looked very rough. His eyes were open as wide as possible. There were two guards escorting him. He was brought in front of the monitor so that Judge Sherry could speak directly to him. She began to read off the reason this guy was in prison. I will not even attempt to quote the entire list of charges she read, but I will give a little overview. Judge Sherry said, "Mr. you are at this hearing for the following charges; assault with the attempted murder, robbery, assault with the intent to cause bodily harm, carrying an illegal weapon" and as she continued, Mr. interrupted her. Mr. said judge I am innocence of everything you said and also the things that you will say. Mr. said I did not do anything and all these charges are made up by the government and my ex-wife. Judge Sherry was trying to stop him from talking, for she was not finished. Mr. would not shut up. Then the guards attacked him and held him down. Mr. went absolutely berserk. Mr. began to curse the judge and fight the guards. The guards called for medical personnel to give Mr. some type of drugs. When Mr. heard about the doctor, he got worse. This was like something you see at the movies. Because the two guards could not contain Mr., more guards came in. The guards wrestled with Mr. Finally, they got him under control and begin to drag him out of the remote courtroom. Mr. was hollering at the top of his voice. Mr. kept screaming about the government and his ex-wife and things that were far more unusual then I will write today.

After about ten minutes of trying to bring order to the remote courtroom, we were finally able to continue. A number of prisoners went before the judge before me and things were going well. Judge Sherry would read off the charges and set the bail, then ask for the next person. Then an older guy went before the judge. Let us call him Tom. I had spoken to Tom last night and found that Tom was arrested for taking furniture out of a house he was renting. He received a letter to report to court concerning this matter. When he came to court, they arrested him and put him in jail. Now Tom went up before Judge Sherry. She read the charges and then asked the prosecutor, "Why is this man in jail? He did not do anything." Judge Sherry asked Tom, "Whose furniture were you taking from the house?" Tom said, "The furniture was mine. My lease was up and I was just there to pickup my household goods. I moved everything out of the house. The next thing I know I am here in prison." Judge Sherry told Tom to pay thirty dollars and go home. Then all hell broke loose. The prosecutor asked Judge Sherry for a sidebar. They talked for about five minutes and then Judge Sherry asked Tom to explain the attempted murder charge that the prosecutor had brought to her attention. Tom broke down and starting crying. Tom said I was cleared of those charges in 1994. How a charge from 1994 could have shown up on Tom's file who knows. Judge Sherry was a little confused and asked the prosecutor to look into this matter more closely. About ten minutes went by as other cases were being considered. The whole time Tom is just in shock.

Tom was about four feet three inches tall and prison was not going to be a good place for him. Then Judge Sherry called Tom back up to talk to him. It was found that the whole thing was a computer error. In fact, Tom's charges had been dropped for over twenty years. I tell this story because there are so many people in the prison system for just errors in the system. Judge Sherry told Tom you are free to go because she was dismissing all charges. She told Tom, "You will have to pay thirty dollars and you can go home." He was so happy! I had prayed so much for Tom. Of the first twenty to twenty five inmates that went before Judge Sherry, I would say she set bail for twenty of them. If they could pay bail, they could go home. I must tell one more story before I get to my visit with Judge Sherry.

There was a guy whom we will call Mike and his turn to meet the judge had come. Mike went before Judge Sherry and was sworn in. The judge asked him if he knew his charges. Mike said he did not. Mike said he was at home and the sheriff came by to talk with him. As they were talking, the sheriff told Mike that there was a warrant for his arrest. Mike was shocked by this announcement. So Mike asked the sheriff what he was being charged with. The sheriff told Mike, "You are being arrested for stealing a car." Mike said this must be a mistake for he had not stolen a car. Therefore, the Sheriff told Mike I have to take you to jail. Little did Mike know that he was being brought to the Federal Prison. Mike told the Judge Sherry his story. Then Judge Sherry told Mike that a complaint had been submitted to the court concerning him stealing a car. Mike asked who made the complaint. Judge Sherry told him the car dealership's name. Mike said, "This can't be true!"

Judge Sherry told Mike before I set your bail tell me what do you have to say about this case. Mike said, "About two months ago I purchased a car from this dealership. I went and purchased the insurance for the car because they would not let me pickup the car until I got the insurance. I gave the dealer a one thousand dollar down payment when I picked up the car. After about three days, the dealership called me to tell me the financing did not go through. They asked me to bring the car back. So I took the car back to the dealership and they gave me the down payment back."

The judge asked Mike could you prove this. Mike said yes I have all the receipts at home. Judge Sherry told Mike to call someone at his house to bring the papers and she would have court for him tomorrow. Mike asked if he really had to stay in prison for another night. Judge Sherry said yes because you have to meet court before I can let you out. Mike then asked, "How much is the bail?" The judge said, "Bail will be twenty percent of the price of the car, which was about three thousand dollars. Mike knew he would have to survive another night in prison. This sounds crazy, but this happens all the time. I am estimating that at least 25% of the people in jail are here because they are caught in the system.

Now it was my time to go before Judge Sherry. I had waited seventeen days for this moment. I had resigned from my job. I had failed two classes toward my Master's degree. I had lost seventeen days of my life and finally I was about to find out why. Judge Sherry asked me to state my name and address. I told her my name and that I lived in Pleasant Grove, Utah. Judge Sherry said, "Utah is a long way from here. Why would you be in my court?"

I told Judge Sherry, "I was picked up on my way to work and I have been in jail for seventeen days." Judge Sherry quickly realized that I did not belong in prison. Judge Sherry noticed how I carried myself when speaking to her.

She said, "Let me look at your charges and see what we can do to get you out of jail." Judge Sherry reviewed my case and said, "You were supposed to show up for court over a year ago. Why did you miss court? All you had to do was show up for court and you would have never gone to jail." I told her that I had no idea that I had a court date over a year ago. I left Louisiana about fourteen months ago and moved to Utah. Judge Sherry said, "There was a summons sent to your address." She stated the address. I told her, "I had closed that office fourteen months ago and would not have been able to receive the summons." I told her I did have a forwarding address but I never received any word from the court. Judge Sherry said the summons could not be forwarded anyway. What we do in a case like yours is issue a bench warrant for a person not showing in court on the scheduled date. We know that the person will be picked up somewhere in the United States. Judge Sherry then said, "I am sorry for the things you have gone through but this is how the system works." Then she said, "Let me read your charges and set your bail. If you can pay the bail, you can go home today but we will not be able to fly you back to Utah. You will have to do that at your own expense." Lord knows these words from Judge Sherry were the greatness words I had heard in a long time. I did not care what the amount of the bail was; I knew I could get it. Then she said you owe the bank for a returned check and there were two checks cashed at a store from a construction company. She asked me did I own the company that issued the checks. I told her I did and that I would have paid these items if I had known about it. Judge Sherry told me the three checks totaled $8,850.00. My bail was set at $885.00. This was music to my ears! Eight hundred and eighty five dollars and I am out of here. Once I am out of prison, I could find out more about the checks at the store. Debbie had already paid the bank because she was able to get with them. There were no tears or any celebration. I just went back to my seat. Then these words came to mine, "Today is Thursday". It was as if someone whispered it into my ear. Earlier, I wrote about a vision that I had. In the vision, the Lord said to me, "You will be out of jail on Thursday." I thought that the Thursday was a couple of weeks ago, but it was not. I had interpreted the vision incorrectly. Yet the Lord showed me that he delivers exactly on time. We must realize that Heavenly Father's time is not our time. His thoughts are not our thoughts.

Now I know exactly what I would have to do to get out of prison. I just needed the court to be completed. Then I could get on the phone to get the money for the bail. There was about another two hours of cases and finally the judge dismissed the court. I told the guard that I needed to use the phone and he told me to wait. The guards then lined us up to return to the holding cell. Everyone was searched to make sure that we did not pickup anything while we were out of the holding cell. We were all back in the holding cells. The guys were truly acting like fools. They were cursing and now the guards were pissed off. I would not be surprised if they did not allow us to use the phones. It was about 11 am now and time was moving fast. The guards decided we could not use the phones. I was upset about this because if I could just speak to Debbie I could get out of here. I could tell I would not be making any phone calls any time soon. The inmates were fighting. Some of the inmates were creating distractions so others could make drugs from materials picked up when we were out of the cells. I was watching all of this take place and the guards were trying to keep order. Man, this was tough. Another hour had passed and things were getting worse. If I could just make a phone call, I could get out of here.

Now, the guards are calling inmate's names. I wondered why the guards were calling their names. What, they just called my name? They let out about twenty of us from the holding cell. Was this a good thing? We were lined up and standing outside of the building. After the guards told us why we were outside, I knew this was not a good thing. As of this moment, I was officially an inmate of the East Baton Rouge Parrish Prison! This was exactly what I hoped would not happen. Now I would have to leave the holding cell area and be placed in a prison block. My heart skipped a beat. I immediately fixed my mind to feel nothing. My mind was set and anger filled my heart. I knew I had to go to battle and the Lord made it possible for me to find the survival instinct that I had to use many times in my past. I was not sure if these feelings existed in me anymore. However, at the exact moment I needed it, this skill came through. Now I was ready. I said a prayer to my Heavenly Father that I be protected while in this place. I prayed that no one would mess with me. You see, there is a certain evil in man when he feels his life is being threatened. I was at that point right now. I would do whatever it takes to survive in this place. Then all of a sudden, my anger left me. A great calm came over me. A great feeling of peace was what I am feeling. I was very happy for this peace. I knew that anger very well and it was not a good feeling. However, this peace I knew not. I just knew that it came from my Heavenly Father.

The guards directed us on about a half-mile journey into the heart of the prison. Along this half mile walk was fencing about ten feet tall with what looked like blades at the top of the fence. We finally made it to a set of double doors. The guard knocked on the door and another guard opened the doors. There was great commotion going on inside these doors. This is what was called a cell area. Within a cell area were multiple blocks. Each block could hold about 200 men and there were at least ten cell blocks in each cell area. When we entered the doors, it was crazy. The guys within the block were saying the most horrible words to us. I will not write much of what was said because it is not worthy to be written. I stayed focus on what I had to do to survive. The guards took us to a room to show us a movie concerning rape in prisons. The movie discusses things to avoid and situations that were indications of rape possibilities. It was a horrible movie. This is all I will say about it. Then we went into another office where picture ID's were created for us. Then we were given a phone card! How exciting. In my hands was access to the source that could get me out of this place. Now what I needed was a phone, but a phone was not to be, at this time. It was about 1:00 pm. The cooks, who are prisoners, brought us lunch. I do not remember what it was. However, when you get hungry enough, you will eat anything.

We had finished lunch and the guys were acting like fools again! I couldn't blame the guards for their behavior because the inmates pushed the guards to their limits. It always seemed like there was going to be a fight between the guards and the inmates, but the guards were not allowed to hit the inmates. The inmates knew this and this was why they pushed the guards so hard. However, for me this was not cool. I wanted the guards to be as happy as possible and leave me alone. We were now headed to meet the doctor. This was the last step in being admitted into the prison population. I met the doctor but it was not much of a checkup. After everyone completed their checkup, we were taken back in the room where we watched the movie. The guards called out about twenty of us and told us to follow them. They took us down a few hallways away from everyone else. I became concerned that something could happen to us. Finally, we made it to a hallway where no one was located. The guards told us to turn around and face the wall. Then we were told to put our hands on the wall. They patted us down to confirm we did not have anything on us. Then they had us to turn around and face them. The guards had us open our mouths so they could check to confirm we did not have anything in our mouths. Then they told us to take off all of our clothes. So here we were, twenty men, standing in a hallway without any clothes on. The guards checked us in our private area to confirm we were not carrying anything there. Then they told us to turn around and face the wall again. I will not write what they asked us to do. Then we were allowed to put our clothes back on. They had us line up and they assigned us to different cell blocks in the prison. Each cell block housed about two hundred prisoners. As we all separated to go to our cell blocks there was a great fear in some of us, but for some reason I had no fear. I kept reminding myself that this was my only way out of being locked up. This was my seventeenth day being in jail and now I was sure I could make it through whatever awaited me.

I reached my cell block and from this very nice hallway, there in front of me were old yellow looking prison bars. This massive gate opened and I entered into my cell block. The full cell area must have been about sixty yards wide and sixty yards deep. There was sixty yards of steel bars with two openings that opened and closed via a guard pressing a button. The gate or opening would slide to the right to open. It made a very loud noise when it opened and closed, like two massive metal pieces grinding against each other. The guards opened this massive gate and I entered in the cellblock. When the gate closed behind me, I felt like I had just been locked up in a tomb! The place I entered was a huge open area and all of the inmates were in this area. There were TV's, card tables and four telephones. My God, there was a phone! I quickly went over to the phone and called Debbie. I dialed her number and she answered. Her voice was the best sound I had heard in a long time. I told Debbie that I was in Baton Rouge. I had left Utah the day before. Debbie had no idea where I was. She only knew that I did not call her yesterday. After some I love you's and how are you's, I shifted into my, "I have got to get out of jail mode." I focused very intensely on everything I had to tell her. I needed all of her attention because other than Heavenly Father, Jesus Christ and the Holy Ghost, Debbie was the most important person in my life. Debbie would have to step outside of her comfort zone and get me out of prison. Even worse, she was going to have to accomplish this from over nineteen hundred miles away. It was about 3:00 pm now and things were going to have to move quickly to get me out today. Before I hung up the phone I made sure Debbie understood that she had to get me out of prison today at all cost!

I hung up the phone. I began to look around to check out my surroundings. When in an environment like this, I had to know the lay of the land. I needed to know who the players in the place were. Ironically, of the two hundred or so men in this cell block, ninety percent were black. I had just left Utah where ninety percent of the inmates were white. Where I was in Utah was a country club compared to this place. As I said, the open area was at least sixty yards long and twenty yards wide. The inmates did everything in this area. Some were exercising by walking or running around the area. Understand this was all indoors and there were no windows to the outside. Then, there were four sets of large cells that housed the inmates' sleeping quarters. There were about fifty sets of bunk beds in each bay. Each bay was a prison within the prison. Each bay would be locked so that no one could leave the bays during lock down. I tell you this was not a place for the weak at heart. This was not even a place for the strong at heart. In Utah, the guards issued you a bunk. Then they would issue you a bed pad, a blanket and toiletries. Here, at East Baton Rouge Prison, the guards did not issue you anything. I was told to get with the bay leader and ask for a bunk and anything else I needed. Here is the problem: the movie we watched told us to never ask an inmate for anything. The guards who worked with us concerning the issues told us, "Do not accept anything from an inmate. Because when an inmate gives you something, they expect something in return." Now here I am at the cell block and the block guard wants me to ask inmates for favors! Another new inmate, we will call him Bill, he and I decided to work together and provide support to each other. Bill and I went into the sleep area and asked, "Are there any beds available?" One inmate just looked at us and said you will have to find you own bed. I asked him, putting my hand on a bunk, "Is this bunk available?" The inmate said no the bunk was not available. There was not even a mattress on the bed. I knew this inmate was not a person to deal with. Bill asked another inmate about a bed and was told, "You cannot have that bed because it is my second bed." About this time another inmate, I will call Will, showed up and said, "Leave these guys alone." It appeared that Will was one of the players in the cell. Will called a couple of inmates and told them to get us a bed pad and a blanket. Bill and I felt good about this and we had bunks next to each other. Bill was just like me waiting for bail to get out of prison. Now I had a bed but I did not plan to sleep in it for Debbie was working on getting me out by paying bail.

Then the big gate opened. There were other new prisoners being processed into this cell block. I saw the individual and it was Tom! Once Tom entered the gate, he started crying. Tom was in his sixties.

When the gate closed like a tomb, Tom stood at the bars of the gate and would not move. He was so afraid. I felt so sorry for him for this man had no reason being here. I started toward him as he turned and saw me. He came over and I introduced him to Bill. Tom only needed to pay $30 and he could go home. The issue was he had to have someone bring the money to the prison. Tom had not been able to get anyone on the phone. It was now around 4:30 pm. It was time for me to check on Debbie and the progress she has made.

I spoke with Debbie and she told me she was waiting on a bail bondsman to call her back. I almost lost it! I told Debbie do not wait on anyone. Call every bail bondman you can get a number for and never wait on anyone! I really did not want to stay in prison, not even for one more night. Bill, Tom and I hung together for a while. I would mingle with some of the older inmates just to try to learn the lay of the land. Every minute that passed seen like hours. It was dinnertime now and we were preparing to go. We would go based on the bay you lived in because dinnertime is when prison breaks were attempted. There were guards everywhere as we walked down the hallway to the cafeteria. There were men actually hollering at us as if we are women. I stayed focus and would not make eye contact with any of them. We finally reached the dinner hall, I said cafeteria earlier, but this was no cafeteria. We lined up along the wall as other inmates were eating at tables. As we passed a table, you could see that some of these guys have been here for a while. These inmates were the hardcore guys. These guys had been in prison for many years. These guys were the murders, child molesters and other hardcore criminals. Tom and Bill were very much afraid and I felt very much uncomfortable myself. These inmates made a grunting sound, which I knew was some type of communication among them. I wanted nothing to do with these guys yet I watched them closely as they communicated with each other via this language. Finally, we got our food and any food you did not eat, someone wanted it. It was like eating with a group of animals. Finally, dinner was over and we were being escorted back to our bay. I knew that there was some communication going on concerning Bill. Bill could sense this also and begin to tear up. I told Bill, "You can't let them know that they are getting to you." Bill became stronger and resisted his fears. This environment was like the years I played football, the opposing team always tried to intimidate you to throw you off your game. This was the same type of environment but this was no game!

Back in the bay, I was going to call Debbie to get a feel for how much progress has been made. Debbie told me she had a bail bondman and had sent the money. The bail bondman also needed someone in Baton Rouge to sign all documents and be responsible for getting me to court when my date came. I asked Debbie for the phone number of the one person who I knew would help me. I called Robert. Robert and I had been very good friends and had done great work with young men and scouting in the Church. I knew to call him for the Lord spoke his name to my spirit. I called Robert and gave him all the details I had and asked him to call Debbie. Now it was about 6:00 pm and the guards had just released two men, whose bail had been posted. I was glad to see them leave but I wanted to get out of here myself.

I really prayed that Tom could get out for this place was not going to work for him. Bill had already had his dad try to post bail for him also. However, time continued to pass slowly and all I could do is continue to wait. Seven pm had come and gone and still I waited to hear the guard call my name to leave. I knew things were in the works, but when you have been locked up for seventeen days, you can only think of getting out. This was the one time I had no control of anything. I must say when you have no control of your life it is a horrible feeling. I was watching a Thursday night football game, but what I was really watching was the clock. It was nine pm now and there was still no word. I called Debbie but I did not want her to hear the desperation in my voice. I was not holding up well as time continued to pass. It was now ten pm and Tom was crying again. He had made numerous phone calls and had not been able to reach his niece. She was the only one he knew that could post bail for him. The guards announced that we couldn't use the phones anymore tonight. I felt a sense of despair knowing that I would not be able to use the phone and my life was in the balance without me having any control. The guards were making another announcement for people who were getting out. This time they called Bill. I was so happy for him but I hated to lose him. Now I was all alone for Tom was in another bay. It was eleven pm and time to go to bed. This was not good at all. I went to my bed. All of my fight was leaving me. All of my hope was leaving me. I had nowhere to turn. I was so alone. I was laying in my top bunk searching for something in me to give me some hope and peace. Hope and peace had left me. Then I heard this strange sound. I looked over and the inmates about three bunks from me were making drugs. I didn't know how this was possible. However, I knew I had to get out of this area. There were about twenty rows of beds and I was in bunk set number 20 near the back of the bay. I did not wait. I got my blanket and moved to the first row in the bay, right next to the prison bars. I ran into Will as I was moving. Will stopped me and then asked me a strange set up question. Will asked, "Are you moving up front?"

I said, "Yes, I am."

Will said, "Moving is a great idea, because those guys will be busted very soon." Then Will asked me, "Are you a Mormon?"

I told him, "Yes, I am."

Bill then said," I could tell when I first saw you. You all have a way of carrying yourselves."

I asked Bill, "What religion do you practice?"

Bill said, "I am non-denominational." Bill's last words to me were, "Man, take care of yourself. It can get tough in here."

I moved to the front bunk and put all of my stuff there. I got into bed and tried to sleep. I was a beaten man. My hope was gone. All of my strength was gone. For seventeen days, I had been beaten mentally. For the last forty-eight hours, I had been physically beaten. My body was tired. My brain was tired. As I lay here in my bunk, I could barely say these words in my heart. "Father, I cannot go any further. I have fought all I can. I am truly a beaten man both physically and mentally. Let this night go well. Thou has brought me this far and I have given all that I have. Bless Debbie, AJ, Kenneth, Tiffany and my grandkids. I cannot fight any longer for my spirit is broken. Strengthen me, Father, for I must rest now. Protect me in my weakness. In the name of Jesus Christ, I pray, Amen."

As tears flowed down my face and my eyes begin to close, I heard the most unbelievable thing. "Kinnith Holloway, pack your stuff you are going home," the guard said. I sat up in my bunk and glanced at the clock. It was eleven forty five. I was not sure if I was dreaming or awake. The guard announced it again, "Kinnith Holloway, get you stuff and report to the guard office." I said to myself, "Thank you, Dear Heavenly Father!" For a man with no energy, I jumped from the top bunk to the floor. One inmate asked, "Could I have your socks?" I told him, "You can have everything I have with me. " Somehow, at this moment my body and spirit were renewed.

I quickly headed to the guard's office. The prison bars opened to allow me to leave the bay where all the beds were. I walked from that point about twenty yards to the next set of prison bars, which opened as soon as I reached them. I walked through these bars and heard them close like the sound of a tomb. The guard asked me, "Where is your stuff?"

I told the guard, "I left everything."

The guard said, "That's fine, you can leave." I walked another twenty to thirty feet to the main door to the prison block. The door opened and I stepped into the hallway. There, another guard met me. The huge metal door, to the prison block, closed behind me like a door to a tomb. The guard escorted me to the front prisoner holding area, which I spoke of earlier in the book. I watched many people brought into prison while I waited to be released. This process took about ninety minutes, but it seemed like days. Finally, all of the processing was over. The prison guard said to me, "You can now leave East Baton Rouge Parish Prison." It was finally over. I thanked my Heavenly Father for watching over me.

When I came out of the prison gates, I had no idea if someone was waiting. I did not have any money and no ID. When I walked out of the gate, I saw a car light flash. I knew who it was. It was Robert. He and Debbie had gotten together over the phone and made everything happen to get me out of prison. I thanked him. Robert took me to his house. He asked me if I needed any food. I told him not right now. I went and showered for about an hour trying to wash the prison off me.

For seventeen days, I had been a prisoner in a jail in Utah and in East Baton Rouge Prison in Louisiana. However, not once in this whole ordeal did I blame anyone for my situation. I knew that my Heavenly Father and Jesus Christ knew my situation. I knew that they knew me personally and would never leave my side. I knew I was never alone and that my Heavenly Father would strengthen me in my time of need. I knew that this was a test, for me, and that I had to endure it. Now that this one test was over, I knew there would be many more. Now, I had to get home to Debbie and rebuild my life for I had lost much. This had been maybe the toughest 17 days of my life. Not because of the things I had to endure, but because of the unknown. Not knowing why I was arrested. Not knowing that I was going to jail. Not knowing how long I would be in jail. Not knowing how I was to survive in the jail environment. Not knowing how or when I would lose my job. Not knowing how big of a financial loss I would take. It was tough not knowing how your wife would survive without you being there. Not knowing your standing in Church. Not knowing the days of the week. Not knowing who was on your right or your left or who is front or behind you. You see, not knowing was a powerful thing. It was the most powerful force I have ever faced!

Now I tell you a secret that should not be a secret. I was not alone in jail. I knew who was on my left and on my right. I knew who was in front of and behind me. I knew that I had a friend who was with me every minute of every day for 17 days. He was with me in my lowest times, which were many. He was with me in my highest times, which were few. He was with me when my heart felt great pain and sorrow, and He lifted me up. When despair gripped my mind and my spirit, He was there to give me peace. When great hope turned to great sorrow, Jesus Christ was there to lift my spirit. When there seemed to be no way out, He was there to shine a light for me to take one more step. When the court told me that I should be prepared to stay in jail for six weeks and my heart cried out with great pain for my family, He was there to steady by heart.

I could have given up many times. There were many times that Satan whispered in my ear, "You are alone and fear is your only friend." Yet I would call upon the Lord and with great power, Satan's whispers would be taken away. The power of the Lord's priesthood was far greater than the whispers of fear from Satan. Remember that a Father will defend his children. "Know you not that we are children of God." If my child is in trouble, I will come and fight for my child. Know then that you are a child of God and He will come and fight for you. However, you must align yourself with Him. I am no great man, yet just as a mother sees her child as the greatest among children, so does our Heavenly Father see you and I in that same light. Oh how great are we in His heart! Fear not! Stand still! Ask your Father who is in heaven for that which you need. He will manifest the answer to your needs in your heart. You take action on that answer from your Heavenly Father and He will lead you, step by step, to your solution.

Chapter 26

We had been back from Utah for a couple of days. I knew we would see the missionaries soon. I did not talk to Debbie concerning what was on my mind. I spent the next two days reviewing everything concerning religions, not just Christianity, but all religions of the world. Could the Church of Jesus Christ of Latter Day Saint have within its hands the restored gospel of Jesus Christ? How could this be true? I couldn't prove this church wrong. All other Christian churches or denominations had many flaws. These flaws were caused because the Gospel of Jesus Christ must be restored. Without a restoration of the Gospel of Jesus Christ, no church or denomination had the information needed to answer the weaknesses of the religion. Now add the Book of Mormon and the other scriptures contained in the Church of Jesus Christ of Latter Day Saints and all the weaknesses of the Bible were no more. Now I felt like the people who were there when Jesus was on the earth. So many people rejected Jesus because he did not fit the status quo of the time. The Pharisees and Sadducees were the religious leaders of their day, just as the Preachers and Ministers represented the religious leaders of today. Both groups of leaders became very wealthy via religious teaching. I would not discuss this any longer. I would join the Church of Jesus Christ of Latter Day Saints.

It was time! As always, the missionaries knocked on the door. Debbie invited them in. They were so excited to see us. We had missed them also. Little did they know this was going to be a surprising night for them and Debbie. The missionaries began asking us a few questions about our trip to Utah. I was not very interested in what they were asking. My mind was slow and my heart was heavy. I began to seek ways to get the missionaries to understand that I was ready to be baptized, yet I did not want them ask me. Erin had become very close to me. Jennie had spoken to me spirit to spirit. Could I reach out to them and express the feelings of my heart? Then a simple thought come to mine. I spoke these words to the missionaries, "If I was going to be baptized, I would do it on the coming Saturday."

Sister Pickett noticed what I was saying. She simply said, "If you want to be baptized on that day, then you can."

I said okay let's do it on that date. I have no idea how anyone in that room felt. I do know that there was a great power that existed in the room. This was not an overwhelming power but a soothing power of peace. The date was set. For the first time, I was going to join a church!

I spent the week before the baptism date studying the Bible and Book of Mormon. Every weakness I found in the Bible was strengthened by the Book of Mormon. I did not want to make a mistake in joining a church. I continued throughout the week to find flaws in the Bible. Yet the Book of Mormon would correct the flaws. These two books together created an unbeatable combination.

Now the day for my interview came. I had no clue what this interview concerned. After the interview, I understood. This interview was to confirm that I was ready to be baptized. The interesting thing was that this interview has nothing to do with the interviewer. The interview was for me to decide if I was ready. I was ready.

The day was here. I was totally at peace. I had done my homework. This was not a decision made after studying with the missionaries for about three months, this decision began when I was twelve years old. My mother came to me when I was twelve and stated, "You are twelve years old now. You can now decide which church to join." The next twenty-eight years I searched for the power that controlled the universe. I searched for Him in every Christian denomination and did not find Him. I went to a tree line to call Him out directly and did not find Him. I searched many of the world religions and I found the way to find God. The Quran (Islamic Scripture) gave me the first clue. The way was Jesus Christ. Without the Quran, I would have never considered being a Christian. Now I knew that Jesus was the way to God. Yet no Christian Church had the information I needed to find the Church of Jesus Christ. Although these Christians are great people and love Jesus Christ, they needed the true gospel to be restored to the earth. The same was true concerning the Israelites when they were in Egypt. The same was true with the Jews when Jesus came to the earth. Therefore out of pure love for His children, Heavenly Father had restored his Gospel yet again. Now I was about to be baptized into the Church that had the restored gospel!

We were in the church and there may have been twenty people in the building. I was not sure what to expect so I was watching everything. There was an opening prayer and some short talks. The curtain opened to reveal the baptismal font. I entered the baptismal font from one side and Gus Stanback entered from the other side. The baptism took place. Then the missionaries sang, "I am a child of God." It was a beautiful song. Now I was waiting for something the missionaries promised me, the Gift of the Holy Ghost. The next day I was to receive this gift. Now please check the Bible. You will find that the Holy Ghost does visit people at times. Then it leaves them. What this Gift of the Holy Ghost is the ability to have the Holy Ghost with you at all times. In the Bible, someone who has the authority to do so gives this gift to a person. John the Baptist baptized many. Yet none of them was given the gift of the Holy Ghost for John the Baptist did not have the authority to do so. The gift of the Holy Ghost was given to Jesus directly from our Heavenly Father. You should ask yourself why is this? Then study the Bible and find out why for yourself.

It was a long day and night waiting for the time to receive this gift of the Holy Ghost.

The time was here. I was to get the gift of the Holy Ghost. I would test what the missionaries had told me. One of the things the missionaries stated that the Holy Ghost would do is assist me in seeing and understanding the scriptures better. They told me other things about this gift of the Holy Ghost, yet I wanted to test this theory of understanding the scriptures better. The Brethren put their hands on my head and gave me the gift of the Holy Ghost. This is exactly as it was done in Bible. Once the gift was given, I felt nothing. The rest of the day went great, yet I wanted to go home and test this gift. Finally, church was over and we were headed home.

Once we got home, we ate a great dinner. Debbie loved to cook a big meal on Saturday for Sunday. She did a great job again on this Sunday. I played with AJ the rest of the day. I decided to start reading the Bible late that night. Debbie and AJ had gone to bed. It must have been around 1:00 am and I was still reading the Bible. Then the strangest things began to happen. The words of the Bible began to lift from the pages. The words of the Bible hovered in the air above the page! This was such an unbelievable thing. I could still read the words as they floated in the air. Everything was so clear. My understanding of the scriptures had increased greatly. I knew that the Holy Ghost had opened my mind and heart to a better understanding of the scriptures. I reached to touch the words but it was as if my hand went through the words. Therefore, for a few verses I was able to read the words as they hovered in the air. Then I went to tell Debbie what I had just experienced. I am not sure what Debbie thought of this. This never happend to me again, yet this was a great thing. My understanding of the scriptures was so much better. Even today, this gift of understanding still exists. Everything was exactly as Jennie and Erin had said. Finally, around 3:00am I went to sleep.

Chapter 27

The next morning was a Monday. Since I owned a computer store, I did not have to be at work at any certain time. The week went great. Debbie had not joined the Church of Jesus Christ of Latter Day Saints yet. Therefore, the missionaries were coming to our home to teach Debbie. Erin asked me, "We know Debbie knows the gospel is true, why doesn't she join the church?" I told the missionaries that Debbie had been a member of the Baptist faith all of her life. It was always difficult for someone to leave his or her traditions. I told the missionaries that Debbie just needed more time. Let me touch on traditions and history, just for a second with a focus on Blacks and Christianity in America.

Blacks were not Christian when we arrived in America. As slaves, Blacks were not allowed to attend any Christian church. Every denomination of Christianity discriminated against black people. In fact, Christianity was used to assist in keeping Blacks as slaves. As Blacks became more familiar with Christianity, via the underground, they wanted to attend the church, yet Blacks were not allowed to attend White Christian churches. Once slavery was over in theory, Whites would not allow Blacks to attend their churches. In order for us to attend a church, the former slave masters would allow the blacks to practice some form of religion based on the former slave master's belief. This was where the Black tradition of Christianity began, yet we were not allowed to join the true Baptist church or any other denomination. Therefore, "slave" Christian churches were created. The only church that openly allowed Blacks to join was the Church of Jesus Christ of Latter Day Saints. Please check your history. I am discussing the early 1800s. Find out how we, as Blacks, had been treated by religious denominations we hold so dear today.

Debbie finally decided to break from her traditions and join the Church of Jesus Christ of Latter Day Saints. I was able to baptize her because I held the proper authority to do so. I held the Aaronic Priesthood. The same priesthood that John the Baptist held. Therefore, by that authority I was able to baptize Debbie. Now I did not have the authority to bestow upon Debbie the gift of the Holy Ghost. Check your Bible and you will find that many disciples could baptize people, yet only a few could bestow the gift of the Holy Ghost. Soon Debbie had the gift of the Holy Ghost bestowed upon her. The following week we were set to go to the temple in Baton Rouge, Louisiana. Review your scriptures and learn about temples. Our week went great. Things began to get better in our business and I could see us finding a way to make it to just under broke. Now the Saturday was here for us to attend the temple. We drove about a hundred and forty miles to the Baton Rouge, Louisiana Temple. At the temple, we would perform special ordinances for the living and the dead. This is all I will write about the temple at this time.

Now I will tell you how Satan works and how the Lord made moves to help us. I was sitting in my office on a Monday. Around ten o'clock a person walked into my store. He was a local preacher. He asked if he could speak with me. This was not an issue for me. I had spoken with hundreds of preachers over the last 20 years. This man began with these words, "I hear you have joined the Mormon Church and I am here to save you from them." This was very surprising to me. My thought was, "Why should you care what I do?" I did not speak a word for I had to listen to understand what this preacher's message concerned. He went on to say that the Mormons were a cult and would really lead me down the wrong road. I stopped him and asked, "Who are these Mormons you speak of?"

He asked, "You did join the Mormon Church?"

I said, "I am unsure of the Mormon Church you speak of, yet I did join the Church of Jesus Christ of Latter Day Saints."

You see, I did not know that the members of the Church of Jesus Christ of Latter Day Saints were called Mormons. Therefore, the preacher went on to give me specific reasons why he felt it was a mistake for me to join this church. I listened to him, for my mom taught me many years ago to listen to people. My dad taught me that I should always make my own decision after listening to people. Therefore, I did listen.

The preacher went on. "The Mormons worship the devil. The Mormons discriminate against Blacks. The Mormons do not allow Blacks to hold the priesthood. The Mormons do not allow Blacks to go into their temples." It will take up a chapter of this book to tell all things he said. Then he suggested that he could help me get away from the Mormons. I am thinking, "What is this guy talking about?" However, to honor my Mother, I did listen. Then he stated, "We will help you, yet you must get away from the Mormons right now. I have some of my friends coming by later today to help you." I thought very little about what he had said as he left.

About two hours later, another preacher shows up. This time I was busy, yet to him saving me from the Mormons was very important. Again, to honor my Mother, I stopped what I was doing to listen to this preacher. This preacher recited the same things as the other minister except in more detail. He must have gone on for about thirty minutes before I stopped him. I said to him, "Let me answer some of your questions." I stated to the preacher, "You said that Blacks could not hold the priesthood in the Church of Jesus Christ of Latter Day Saints?"

The preacher said, "That is correct Blacks cannot hold the priesthood in that church." I said to the preacher, "I hold the Aaronic Priesthood. Could you be mistaken concerning the priesthood?"

I then asked the preacher, "Did you say that Blacks were not allowed to enter the Mormon temples?"

This preacher stated, "That is correct. Blacks cannot enter into these devil worshipping houses."

I told the preacher that I had just attended a Mormon temple a couple of days before. I told the preacher that he must be mistaken. He continued his attack as if he did not hear a word I had just said. Therefore, I stopped him before he could continue another thirty minutes of being ignorant. I said to the preacher, "Let me ask you a question." I gave him an overview of some of the things Jesus did while he was on the earth. Such as healing the sick, preaching the gospel and other good things. I asked the preacher, "Would you agree that Jesus' main statement was 'come see?' Then there were people who came to see. Jesus would then teach and heal the people who came to see." The preacher agreed. Then I asked the preacher, "If you were living at the time Jesus walked the earth and Jesus said, 'Come see.' Would you have gone to see Jesus?" The preacher stated, "I would have went to see Jesus and helped him spread the gospel." I said, "That is great, now may I ask you another question?" I held the Book of Mormon in my hand. I moved the book toward the preacher. Then I asked him, "Here, will you read this book. All I am asking is will you 'come and see'?"

The preacher immediately responded, "I will not read it for that book is of the devil."

As he was about to continue, I stopped him and stated, "You would not have gone to see Jesus Christ either. It is people like you who almost made me miss Christianity."

You see we should not fear reading a book. For how else can a person understand a message but to go see and hear. The preacher responded toward the Book of Mormon, exactly the way the Pharisees and Sadducees responded toward the gospel of Jesus Christ. I find it to be very disturbing when the "keepers of the word" (the ministers and preachers today; the Pharisees and Sadducees of old) are so afraid to even read a book! These leaders will read all the books of men, yet if a book says it is of God, these same leaders will not read it. Even worse, they stop others from reading it. Then this preacher asked me to come to his church. I told him I would attend his church, in return I requested that he read the Book of Mormon. He agreed.

Later, I attended the preacher's church. The service was the same as all other churches I had attended in the past. After church, the preacher asked Debbie and I to come to his office. We went to his office for I have no fear of any religious person, nor did I fear the devil. Once we were in his office, he pulled out all type of books, tapes, CDs and many other anti-Mormon materials. His objective was to show me that the Church of Jesus Christ of Latter Day Saints was of the devil. I let him go on for about thirty minutes with all of his materials and negative talks about the Church of Jesus Christ of Latter Day Saints. Finally, I had to stop him for I could not allow him to condemn himself and Christianity any further. I took the Bible and asked that we read 1st Corinthians Chapter 15 together. I will not go over the complete chapter but I will discuss some of the verses in this chapter, mainly verses 18-29. I asked the preacher to explain these verses. He began to explain the verses and was doing a great job. Then he reached verse 29, which states,

"29 Else what shall they do which are baptized for the dead, if the dead rise not at all? Why are they then baptized for the dead?" (KJV)

The preacher stopped and quickly said, this is a mystery of God and man is not to know what this verse means. I asked him to read this verse because he had just spent fifteen minutes condemning the Church of Jesus Christ of Latter Day Saints for practicing this ordinance. The preacher felt that the Mormons made up this concept. I knew that this preacher only read the Bible to get just enough information for his performances on Sundays. You see he had never read this scripture before. Therefore, he did what all preachers I have met do when they do not have an answer. They use the, "It is a mystery" card. I asked the preacher, "Why do you not accept verse 29 in the same context as you accepted verses 1-28? I am sure Paul meant exactly what he said in verse 29 as well all of the other verses." The preacher did not say a word. I sensed his frustration and suggested that we read another scripture. The scripture that we read next was Revelation 14:6.

"**6** And I saw another angel fly in the midst of heaven, having the everlasting gospel to preach unto them that dwell on the earth, and to every nation, and kindred, and tongue, and people,"

I did not ask the preacher what he thought about this scripture. I said to him, "the answer to the mysteries you find in the Bible can be found in the everlasting gospel that John prophesied about in the scripture. Now if someone claims these prophesies have been fulfilled, would you want to find out about this claim?"

The preacher did not say a word. He just sat there, in his own office, with nothing to say. I asked, "Pastor, will you now read the Book of Mormon as you agreed?"

The preacher stated, "No I will not."

Debbie and I left and no other preacher in that area ever spoke to me again.

September 11, 2001 occurred. Everything had gone wrong for us over the last two years. We lost the computer store and all of our money. Therefore, we went from retired to broke in less than three years. Yet we were the richest we had ever been, for we had found the True Gospel of Jesus Christ. Let me rephrase that. Heavenly Father decided to take two young girls from their homes in Utah. He requested of them to give up eighteen months of their lives to go to a foreign land. There, He knew they would find Debbie and me. Jesus Christ, my brother, knew who to send for He knew Debbie and me.

Debbie and I moved from Ferriday, Louisiana to Baton Rouge, Louisiana. Six months later, Debbie and I were able to complete our endowments. We were sealed in the temple to each other for time and eternity. On that same day, our son, AJ, was sealed to Debbie and me. We have served in many callings in the Church. Now, I will tell you a story. I went to the Baton Rouge Temple to perform a baptism for my dad. When I was baptized for my dad, a vision opened up in my mind. There was a very long, winding river. I saw my dad on one side of the river. He reached out his hand to me as I was standing on the other side of the river. I reached out my hand and shook his hand. My dad looked me in the eyes, and then nodded his head. Then the vision closed. Many great blessings have occurred in our lives that I will not write about here. However, there was no greater blessing then to have the opportunity to see our son, AJ, serve a mission for the Lord.

This is a message from Elder AJ Holloway as he closes out his mission!

Well, it is my last 3 days in the field. It has been the best experience of my life and laid a foundation that I know could not have come any other way. It is amazing how God designs the Gospel to test and stretch us. What I have really learned on my mission is that there is no other way. Only the Gospel can save us. Only the Gospel can refine us. Only the Gospel can change us. I have seen firsthand how the Lord moves mountain in our lives to help us change. I have also seen how we choose whether or not we want those mountains moved. He loves us so much that He gives us a choice. He understands how much we can choose and how much we can gain or lose from our choices. I have learned that the Gospel of Jesus Christ as restored by God through the prophet Joseph Smith Jr. is the only Gospel that contains the fullness of Christ and our Father. It is the only Gospel that can exalt mankind and bring out God's eternal purposes. I have learned about who we really are: sons and daughters of God with the potential to be exactly like Him. It amazes me that God our Father would be so loving as to provide a Plan by which we can be exalted as He is. It's amazes me that He wants us to be so much more than just empty worshipers but that He wants us to be as He is and enjoy the life He has. God is not a mystery and He has never intended to be. He gives us little by little until we know Him perfectly.

What a joy it has been to be a front-line soldier for the Lord Jesus Christ and yes, it has felt just like war sometimes. I have been "troubled on every side, yet not distressed", "perplexed, but not in despair" and "persecuted, but not forsaken". (2 Cor 4:8-9) It has been hard but worth it. The defeats make the victories that much sweeter. I am excited to live as a disciple for rest of my life and to keep being a part of the work of salvation. I promise you that things are meant to be tough and they produce the greatest faith. Always remember the words of Peter. When asked by Christ, "Will ye also go away?", he responds with the most profound and faithful answer of all: "Lord, to whom shall we go? thou hast the words of eternal life." That testimony of Christ and His gospel is the glue that will hold everything together for time and all eternity.

Stay strong and fight the good fight of faith!

Elder Holloway
— with A.J. Holloway.

Chapter 28

This book is not about my seventeen days in jail. The book is not about the many denominations of Christianity I have studied. This book is about an eighteen-year-old young man who wanted to know the truth concerning what his mother believed. He saw her faith in something that did not seem possible to him. Christianity, as far as he was concerned, did not add up. In order to understand something, you must investigate that something. This is exactly what he did. Over the next three years, this young man studied all the denominations of Christianity. When he was unable to find what he was looking for by studying the denominations, he turned to studying the complete Bible. From this study, he concluded that there was something missing from the Bible. In his own words, "It appears that by just studying the Bible, Christians cannot achieve the goal that they are attempting to achieve."

In this youth's quest to find the truth concerning Christianity, he decided to ask God directly. To do this, he went to a line of trees to attempt to speak with God. He found that this concept did not work for him. He decided from this failure that Christianity was not true. He turned his focus to studying religions of the world. He studied Hinduism, Jainism, Buddhism and many other world religions. Finally, he studied Islam, and then everything changed. In the Quran, the Islamic scripture, he found something interesting concerning Jesus Christ. He wrote, "I found in the Quran a witness that Jesus Christ was born, lived, died, came back to life and never died again." This put him on a quest to find out if any other religion made the same claim. He did not find any other religion that made that claim. He wrote, "Now in my hands I have two witnesses that Jesus was born, lived, died, came back to life and never died again. Those witnesses are the Holy Bible and the Quran."

From this point, he began to study the Bible again to find what he had missed the first time he studied it. From the first page of Genesis to the last page of Revelation, he studied, documenting as he went. Upon concluding his studies, he still came to the same conclusion, "Something is missing from the Bible." Yet he knew that the key to everything in life focused on the one man who, he wrote, "was born, lived, died, came back to life and never died again. I know of many people who were born. I know of many people who have lived. I also know of many people who have died. There is nothing to worship here. However, if a man can die and come back to life and never die again, I want to know more about him." This young man spent months trying to find a solution to what he called, "things missing from the Bible." Finally he thought, "What questions would need to be answered to make the Bible true?" Over the next few weeks, he came up with six things or questions that if he could find the answer to, he could become a follower of Jesus Christ. I am going to list the young man's six questions here. Read them. Study them. Then search your Bible for the answers. Ask anyone that you want these questions. Listen to their answers and compare it with the Bible's answers. You will know what to do next.

1. How do I identify the Holy Ghost? Do not spend time thinking about what you have heard from men. Go to the source of the truth, the Holy Bible and search for the answer. You may find that what has been preached to you does not match what the Bible says.

2. Is Heavenly Father and Jesus Christ the same person? Check your Bible. In the Bible is the answer. You do not have to attend college to know the answer. Study your Bible. The Holy Ghost will reveal to you the truth. However, we must seek the answer.

3. Should a minister be paid to preach the gospel that God gave freely to him? What did Abraham charge? What did Moses charge? What did Jesus charge? Search your scriptures and find the truth.

4. Where is my Prophet? I find it very interesting that everyone in the Bible had a prophet and yet I do not have one. Search your Bible and understand the value of Heavenly Father's prophets. Now where is yours? The True Church of Jesus Christ will be led by a prophet.

5. Where is the Temple of God? This one was always interesting to me. The temple is "The House of God." If there is not a temple then where is God's house on earth? Search your scriptures and understand the value of the temple. God has ordinances that are only performed in His Temples. If there is not a temple, then where are the ordinances performed? What are the ordinances that must be performed in God's Temple? If we do not know what these ordinances are then we must not have the fullness of God's Gospel!

6. What happens to a person who lived a good life and died without hearing the Gospel of Jesus Christ? It is taught by many Christians that when we die, we will go to either heaven or hell. Those who accept Jesus Christ go to heaven; all others go to hell. Would you do this to your children, send them to hell simply because you sent (born) them to a country that did not teach of Jesus Christ? A loving Father would never do this. He would create a way to save all of His children. Our Heavenly Father has setup a way for everyone who has ever lived on the earth to return to Him. If you do not know God's plan for those who died without hearing the Gospel of Jesus Christ, then you do not have the Full Gospel of Jesus Christ.

AND THEN...EVERYTHING CHANGED

I searched for the answers to these six questions in order to consider becoming a Christian. If a Church could answer these questions, then that Church would have the "Full Gospel or the Everlasting Gospel of Jesus Christ." The Sister Missionaries were able to answer all of my questions. And then everything changed.

To set up a fireside, please send an email to:
AtEveryThingChanged@gmail.com or call 801.900.1775

May Heavenly Father Bless You!

CPSIA information can be obtained
at www.ICGtesting.com
Printed in the USA
FSOW02n1256120217
30708FS

9 781478 762744